Voiceprint

An anthology of oral and related poetry from the Caribbean

selected and edited by
Stewart Brown
Mervyn Morris
Gordon Rohlehr

with an introduction by Gordon Rohlehr

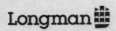 Longman

Longman Group UK Limited
Longman House, Burnt Mill, Harlow
Essex CM20 2JE, England
and Associated Companies throughout the World

Longman Jamaica Limited
P O Box 489
Newport West
Kingston 10
Jamaica

Longman Caribbean (Trinidad)
Boundary Road
San Juan
Trinidad

First published in Longman Caribbean Writers 1989

Set in 9/10 pt Baskerville
Produced by Longman Group (FE) Ltd
Printed in Hong Kong

ISBN 0 582 78629 0

British Library Cataloguing in Publication Data

Voiceprint: an anthology of oral and related poetry from the Caribbean.
(Longman Caribbean Writers).
1. Poetry in English. Caribbean writers, to 1985—Anthologies
I. Brown, Stewart, *1951*—II. Morris, Mervyn, *1937*—III. Rohlehr,
Gordon, *1942*—
811′.008′091821

ISBN 0-582-78629-0

Contents

Introduction

Dreadtalk, Dub, Sermon, Prophesight and Prophesay

Calypso

Pan, Calypso, and Rapso Poems

Parang and Hosay

Monologues

Signifying: Robber Talk

Praise Songs, Prayers and Incantations

Tracing, Curses and other Warnings

Political Manifestos and Satire

Voice Portraits

Word-Songs

Acknowledgements

We are grateful to the following for permission to reproduce copyright material;

the author, Michael Aarons for his poem 'For Indira Gandhi'; the author's agents for the poems 'Man to Pan' and 'Listen Mr Oxford Don' by John Agard; Almo/Irving Music Publications for the songs 'Rat Race' and 'Talkin' Blues' by Bob Marley; Edward Arnold Ltd for the poem 'Ol' Higue' by Wordsworth McAndrew from *Caribbean Poetry Now* ed. by Stewart Brown (pub. Hodder & Stoughton); the author, Edward Baugh for his poems 'Nigger Sweat' and 'The Warner Woman'; the author, Louise Bennett for her poems 'Roas' Turkey', 'Cousin Joe', 'Me Bredda' and 'Cuss-Cuss'; Bogle L'Overture Publications Ltd for the poem 'Language Barrier' by Valerie Bloom and 'Carousel' by Lucinda Roy in *Touch Mi Tell Mi!* by Valerie Bloom; the author, Edward Kamau Brathwaite for his poems 'Stone (for Mikey Smith)', 'Kingston in the Kingdom of this World', 'Cherries' and 'Flutes'; Mrs Kathleen Calliste for the poem '474 Years of Pain and Suffering' and the calypso 'Isms/Schisms' by Leroy Calliste; Jonathan Cape Ltd for the poem 'Hawk' from *The Gulf* by Derek Walcott; Caribbean Contact for the poems 'Kaisoman' by Lasana Kwesi; Caribbean Contact and Writers Union of Trinidad and Tobago for the poem 'Prince Street' by Kasi Senghor; the author, Faustin Charles for his poems 'The Red Robber', 'Carnival' and 'Greenidge'; Chatto & Windus Ltd and Minorities Arts Advisory Service Ltd for the poem 'Mama Dot Warns Against an Easter Rising' from *Mama Dot* by Fred D'Aguiar; The Copyright Organisation of Trinidad and Tobago Ltd for the calypsos 'Deaf Pan Men' by Willard Harris (Relator), *'Bass Man'* by Winston Bailey (Mighty Shadow) and 'Dis Place Nice' by Emerold Phillip (*Brother* Valentino); the author, Christine Craig for her poems 'For Roberta Flack & Sisters' and 'For the Sax Player'; the author, Joseph Cummings for his poem 'A Voice from de Grave'; the author, David Dabydeen for his poem 'Two Cultures'; Faber & Faber Ltd for the poems 'Tales of the Islands: Chapter VI', 'The Spoiler's Return' and 'The Saddhu of Couva' from *Collected Poems* by Derek Walcott; Farrar, Straus and Giroux Inc for the poem 'For Harry Simmons' from *Another Life* by Derek Walcott, © 1973 Derek Walcott; the author, John Figueroa for his poem 'On his Grandmother's Death'; Garland Publishing Inc for the poem 'Litany' from *First Poems* by George Campbell (1981); the author, Dr Michael Gilkes for his poem 'Son of Guyana'; the author, Lorna Goodison for her poems 'Sister Mary and the Devil', 'Road of the Dread' and 'Mother the Great Stones Got to Move'; the author, A L Hendriks for his poem 'Grandmother'; the author, Kendel Hippolyte for his poems 'Zoo Story' and 'Mammon'; the author, Elsworth Keane for his poems 'Brung-skin Gyurl', 'Shaker Funeral', 'Calypso Dancers' and 'Per Capita Per Annum'; the author, Paul Keens-Douglas for his poem 'Jus' Like Dat' from *Tell Me Again* (Keensdee Productions Ltd, Trinidad, 1979); the author, Anthony Kellman for his poem 'Song of Praise'; the author, Cameron King for his poem 'The Country Black Black'; the author, Knolly La Fortune for his poem 'Carnival Rhapsody'; Lawrence & Wishart Ltd for the poem 'My Song is for all Men' by Peter Blackman; the author, John Robert Lee for his poem 'Letter'; the author Mervyn Morris for his poems 'Malefactor (Left)' and 'Malefactor (Right)'; the author, Ian McDonald for his poem 'God's Work'; the author, Anthony McNeill for his poems 'For the D', 'The Catherine Letter I' and 'Ungod on The Day of the Egg'; the author, Roger McTair for his poems 'March February Remembering' and 'Ganja Lady' © Roger McTair 1988; the author, Brian Meeks for his poem 'March 9, 1976'; the author, Pamela Mordecai for an excerpt from the first movement of her poem 'Southern Cross' and her poem 'Last Lines'; New Beacon Books Ltd for the poems 'Mulatta Song' from *I Am Becoming My Mother* by Lorna Goodison (1986), 'Me As Well – The Blackman' from *Foundations* by John La Rose (1966), 'Valley Prince' from *The Pond* by Mervyn Morris (1973); Oxford University Press for the poem 'Chain of Days' from *Chain of Days* by James Berry (1985); the author, Opal Palmer Adisa for her poem 'Ethiopia Under A Jamaican Mango Tree'; Panrun Collective for the poems 'Panrun II' and 'Instant Ting' from *The Whirlwind* by Abdul Malik Decoteau, © Abdul Malik (Panrun Collective London, 1988); the author, Raoul Pantin for his poems 'Pilar' and 'Journey'; the author, Velma Pollard for her poems 'Fly' and 'Screws Loose'; Mrs Iris Roach for the poems 'Hard Drought', 'Verse in August', 'I am the Archipelago' and 'Transition' by Eric Merton Roach; the author, Andrew Salkey for his poem 'Maurice'; the author, Dennis Scott for his poems 'Uncle Time', 'Dreadwalk', 'Apocalypse Dub', 'Lemonsong', 'Guard-ring' and 'More Poem'; the author, Olive Senior for her poem 'The Despatcher'; the author, A J Seymour for his poems 'The Legend of Kaieteur' and 'Tomorrow Belongs to the

People'; the author, P D Sharma for his poem 'Government Memorandum'; the author, Barbara Ferland for her poem 'Ave Maria'; the author, Philip Sherlock for his poems 'Trees His Testament'; Mrs Nerissa Smith for the poems 'Mi Cyaan Believe It' and 'Trainer' by Michael Smith; Sparrow's Hideaway, a division of Sparrow's Enterprises Ltd, for the songs 'Dan is the Man in the Van' and 'Capitalism Gone Mad' by Slinger Francisco (Sparrow); the author, Bruce St John for his poems 'Friends' and 'With Respect'; Uprising Culture on behalf of the author, for the poem 'Book So Deep' by Brother Resistance; Virago Press Ltd for the poems 'Granny in de Market Place' from *Long Road to Nowhere* by Amryl Johnson, © Amryl Johnson 1985 (pub. Virago Press 1985) and 'Invitation' from *The Fat Black Woman's Poems* by Grace Nichols, © Grace Nichols (Printed by Virago Press 1984); the author, Lester Efebo Wilkinson for his poems 'Epilogue . . . 1978' and 'Petit Careme' from *That Man May Live*; Writers Union of Trinidad & Tobago for the poems 'Trini' by Selwyn Bhajan, 'Hey Alfie' and 'Cadence' by Anson Gonzalez, © Anson Gonzalez, from *Collected Poems 1964–1969*, The New Voices, Diego Martin, 1979, 'Down Beat', 'Pan Drama', 'Wreck', 'Shaka's Cycle' by Victor Questel, © Marian Questel, first published in *Near Mourning Ground*, The New Voices, Diego Martin, 1979, 'Absence' by Victor Questel, © Marian Questel, first published in *Hard Stares*, The New Voices, Diego Martin, 1982.

We have been unable to trace the copyright holders in the following and would appreciate any information that would enable us to do so;

the poem 'Memorial Blues for Billie Holiday' by Alec Best; the poem 'Riddym Ravings' by Jean Binta Breeze; the poem 'Canto 1' by Dionne Brand; the poems 'Black Friday 1962' and 'Weroon Weroon' from *Poems of Succession* by Martin Carter (pub. New Beacon Books 1978), 'For Angela Davis' and 'Assassins of the Voice' by Martin Carter; the poem 'Hymn to the Sea' by Frank Collymore; the poem 'Kaleidoscope' by Wayne Davis; the poems 'Electric Eel Song', 'The Mighty Intriguer', 'December 1974: A Lament' by Slade Hopkinson; the poem 'Klickity Klack' by Ras Michael Jeune from *Church and State* (pub. Black Chant Publishers, 1987); the poem 'Sooner or Later' by Bongo Jerry; the poems 'Reggae for Radni' and 'Inglan is a Bitch' by Linton Kwesi Johnson (pub. Race Today); the calypso 'The Devil' by Sedley Joseph (Penguin); the poem 'Hosay' by Christopher Laird; the calypso 'Apocalypse' by Franz Laubkin (Delano); the calypso 'Sea

Water and Sand' by Hollis Liverpool (Mighty Chalkdust); the calypso 'The Gold in Africa' by Neville Marcano (Tiger); the poem 'Still Deh Deh' by Mbala; the poem 'Butta Pan Kulcha' by Mutabaruka; the poem 'Echo' by Oku Onuora; the calypso 'Fountain of Youth' by Theophilus Phillip (Spoiler); the poem 'Graf Zeppelin' by Raymond Quevedo (Atilla the Hun); the calypso 'Take the Meat Out Me Rice' by Aldwyn Roberts (Lord Kitchener).

Introduction

'The Shape of that Hurt'

(i)

It is only since the 1970s that the term 'oral tradition' began to be consistently used in connection with certain developments in West Indian poetry. Before then the debate concerned the viability of 'dialect' as a medium for poetry, and was an extension of the troubled issue of the nexus between education, speech, class, status and power. Creole dialects were thought of as belonging to the semi-literate and poor. To argue, as some linguists did and still do, that Creole is simply another language, neither better nor worse than any other, was to ignore the social and political nature of language. To speak about the vitality and expressiveness of Creole was to sentimentalise warm folksiness without wanting to share in the anguish of its decrepitude, and to display the contempt of a complacent intelligentsia, who secretly wanted to reinforce their superior social status by keeping the mass of the people uneducated.

Nowhere has the 'dialect' versus 'standard' polemic been more bitter than in the question of whether serious poetry can grow out of a dialect base. Since it was widely believed that dialect was a restricted code, incapable of expressing abstract ideas, sublimity or complexities of thought and feeling, the functions permitted dialect were those of drama and energetic folksy humour. While West Indian novelists had from the 1920s begun to reveal the widening possibililties of Creole dialects as flexible literary languages, West Indian poets, with a few notable exceptions, made relatively little use of them. A visible gap also existed between quasi-poetic folk forms such as the mento, chant and calypso, and the formal poetry of the schoolmen. The debate about the status, nature and potential of dialect did little to close this gap, serving rather to harden the prejudices at either edge of the chasm.

One useful concept, however, did emerge, which influenced the direction of literary criticism: that of a 'continuum' stretching between Creole and Standard English, from which speakers naturally selected registers of the language which were appropriate to particular contexts and situations. The notion of a continuum made sense of what West Indian novelists had been doing for some time, that is, exploring the whole range of language and speech registers open to them. The poets also needed to recognize that alternative registers were accessible to them and to liberate, through an openness to all available voices, such word-shapes as these voices might suggest.

If continuum theory revealed a potential for Creole as a language, the concept of an oral tradition made immediately accessible a virtually limitless range of prosodic, rhetorical, and musical shapes, which inevitably became the basis of new making. Roughly parallelling both the folk/urban and the Creole/Standard continua was an aesthetic one:

> . . . stretching between forms derived from an oral paradigm . . . and forms suggested by various aspects of modernist aesthetics . . . While some writers are able to accommodate both extremes with relative ease, others have been involved in an intense dialectic in which the extremes appear as thesis and antithesis . . . The notion of an aesthetic continuum allows us to understand and accept the existence of both types of writer.[1]

This anthology is partly concerned with poetry based on an understanding of the oral tradition. The inclusion of selections from Claude McKay, Louise Bennett, Philip Sherlock, early Arthur Seymour and Elsworth Keane, illustrates the experiments with voice, fable and rhythm that were taking place fifty years ago. These experiments increased in the 1960s, gaining sudden depth with the publication of Edward Kamau Brathwaite's *Rights of Passage*, *Masks* and *Islands* (1967–69). Brathwaite's trilogy, later to be published in a single volume as *The Arrivants* (1973), absorbed and improvised on earlier efforts at orality ranging from Akan traditional drum-poets, through Caribbean pioneers, Afro-American musicians and poets, and the Beat poets. Out of this web of ancestors Brathwaite wove a network of sound-skeins, in which the full folk/modernist continuum was included.[2]

After the appearance of *The Arrivants*, the terms of the aesthetic debate had to change. On the one hand, the issue hardened into an absolute struggle between two opposite camps; on the other, one became aware of the range and versatility of the oral tradition as a source of creative extension into new poetic forms.

The oral tradition is a heritage of song, speech and performance visible in such folk forms as the litanic work songs, chants, battle songs, Queh Queh songs, hymns, thousands of calypsos, mentos and reggae songs, sermons of both the grass-roots and establishment churches, riddles, jokes and word-games. Societies such as Guyana and Trinidad, with their large East Indian communities, possess at least two alternatives to the European models enshrined in the education system. A few calypsos and several songs which blend Hindi and English, suggest that an intercreolization[3] process has been taking place between African and Indian folk elements. The potential of this blend has not been recognized by either community, even though nearly two decades ago musicians such as Joe Harriott, Elsworth Keane, Coleridge Goode and the Johnny Mayer Quintet, had already illustrated the possibilities of fusing Indian classical music and black people's classical music, Jazz.[4]

Music, because it has been the means of preserving linkages between the Caribbean and non European sensibility, has become the container of a wealth of alternative rhythms, a few of which have begun to inform the poetry of the Caribbean. Songs were the Caribbean's first poems, though for a long time, poets limited themselves to the standard ballad style of the Anglo-Scottish tradition. Hence Claude McKay's *Constab Ballads* and a great deal of Louise Bennett were patterned on the iambic tetrametric quatrain shapes of hymns, and Burns's ballads. Prosodic achievement here had to be confined to the tension created through the counterpoint of Jamaica Creole speech rhythms and the fixed metric cage of the stanza. It is in the heightened dramatic situations of Louise Bennett's street poems 'Candy Seller' and 'South Parade Peddler', with their 'tracings' and aggressive performance, that the interplay between voice and metre is greatest.

An illustration of the dominance of the quatrain is seen in the work of Antonio Jarvis from St Thomas, who in 1935 published a small collection of verse entitled *Bamboula Dance*. This title would have led one to expect the shaping influence of the bamboula drums, of Congolese origin, with their warlike rhythms, which were known throughout the Archipelago both before and after Emancipation. One might also have expected Jarvis to draw on the bamboula songs, whose function in St Thomas had once paralleled that of the Kalinda chants and satirical banter songs of mid to late nineteenth century Trinidad and Martinique. This is not the case. *Bamboula Dance* is standard hymn-book stuff, whose culturally biassed content explains its formal limitation.

> Can I in pride mock sad buffoons
> Who ape ancestral circumstance?
> My fathers, too, these thousand moons
> Cavorted in some tribal dance.
>
> I can still feel, when drumbeats call
> The pulsing blood new rhythms take
> As garment-like refinements fall
> Unconscious longings spring awake.
>
> My honoured sire now would say,
> For all his solemn high degrees
> That drums recall Nigerian play
> And drown out later dignities.
>
> Few naked tribesmen yet remain
> To dance the sacred dance for rain.[5]

The poem is a sonnet in iambic tetrameter, and though it speaks of an African heritage which is still sufficiently powerful to produce the 'pulsing new rhythms' of the St Thomas Bamboula dance, and awaken the 'unconscious longings' which lie beneath the flimsy cloak of 'refinements', that heritage of sound, rhythm and orality contributes nothing to its making. Despite its subversive power, the alternative tradition is recognized negatively as the misguided and nostalgic concern of 'sad buffoons/ Who ape ancestral circumstance?' There is a genuine confusion and contradiction here in how 'heritage' is perceived.

Jarvis identifies his father in this poem as a spokesman for Western Atlantic education and civilization, whose 'solemn high degrees', are drowned out by the older Nigerian heritage. Western dignity is defeated by the childishness of an engrained savagery. In another little poem entitled 'Atavistic', Jarvis describes his 'alien sire' as 'Nordic', and himself as the meeting point of contradictory ancestral tendencies.

> I whose dark ancestors played
> Where the Nile's first drop was laid
> Have within me Nordic blood
> Pulsing like the tide at flood.
>
> Dowered by an alien sire
> Is it strange my tropic fire
> Often cools to virtuous fear
> When nice brown girls venture near?

The epithet 'alien' which he applies to his father suggests that the heritage of Nordic blood, here depicted as powerfully alive, is also strangely cold and distant. It represents 'virtue', but it also represents inhibition, the death of Eros, which is illustrated by his inability to respond to the beauty of women of his own ethnicity.

Jarvis thinks in terms of stereotypes which had been established in the European mind centuries before the twentieth[6] and are still present in the Caribbean today. Africa equals drum, naked tribesmen cavorting, play, passion and backwardness; Europe equals refinement, culture, education, intelligence, virtue and self-control. According to the rigid mathematics of such stereotyping which climaxed in the mid-nineteenth century with Arthur de Gobineau's *The Inequality of Human Races*, the psyche of the person of mixed racial heritage became a battlefield of conflicting elements. Since the African aspect of a mixed colonial heritage was under constant official and personal censorship,[7] the 'mulatto of culture' was faced with the choice of either total negation of, or subversive self-identification with the black ancestor. Since progress, thought and enlightenment were thought to be exclusively Western and 'Nordic', and colonial education entrenched and reinforced such prejudice, the Caribbean mulatto of culture was programmed to believe totally in the white ancestor.

The affirmation of the white ancestor and denial or degraded perception of the black one, was most visible whenever the question of an aesthetic arose. The rigidly stereotyped terms of perception described above, lay beneath the bitter arguments concerning West Indian poetry as late as the 1970s. If in 1935 Jarvis could censor the 'new rhythms' engendered in the 'pulsing blood' by the call of drumbeats, with the argument that the New World mulatto had moved beyond the naked tribesmen whose 'sacred dance for rain' had lost its meaning, Eric Roach would bitterly condemn the emergence of these new rhythms in the poetry of the 1970s, employing the same terms as Jarvis.

> Are we going to tie the drum of Africa to our tails and bay like mad dogs at the Nordic world to which our geography and history tie us?

> We have been given the European languages and forms of culture in the traditional aesthetic sense, meaning the best that has been taught, said and done.[8]

Roach wasn't alone in the sentiments he expressed, nor in his declaration that, 'To be a Caribbean English language poet is to be aware of the functions and structure of English verse.'[9] Nor was he singular in his ambivalence towards the 'cultural dominance' of English literature, which he advised the young post-Independence West Indian writer to both 'revere' and 'disdain'. His ambivalence was that of the 1930s mulatto of culture, and like Jarvis's, involved the negation or scornful caricature of the African artistic presence, and the reverent acknowledgement of the European presence, along with a contradictory resentment at the cultural power which the European presence had historically exercised over the colonial person.

Roach's position was rendered even more painful by the anguish which he felt and expressed as a black poet, at the degradation in which black people in Africa, America and the Caribbean were existing. His political position and bitter ethnic loyalties were in harsh conflict with his cultural and aesthetic preferences.

(iii)

If Roach had remained the aesthetic creature of the colonial era, West Indian poetry had not. The alternative tradition, alive enough throughout the colonial period to have required constant censorship by Law, Pulpit and School, had since Independence become the medium of the whole new group of artists, for whom it provided the basis of an indigenous sensibility. The self-censorship of the pre-Independence generations had been the product of, as it had been reinforced by, the legalized censorship of a variety of folk forms. An essential principle of plantation and colonial society, censorship in its various forms, drove the folk tradition into maroonage: stickfighting and Orisha to the provinces, the Baptists to the hills and bushes on pain of prosecution and police harassment,[10] herb-lore and magic to the underground; the dark pagan gods to Catholic and Calvinist versions of hell-fire; waist-movement and buttock-ripple to Dungle, Behind-the-Bridge, Back-O'-Wall penumbra of Jamette, Wahbeen, Robust Man and Jagabat.

Censorship took a serious toll on the folk-consciousness of Trinidad, where even among grass-roots preservers and developers of folk tradition, one could observe curious gaps in sensibility. Shango or Spiritual Baptist worshippers, outlawed by the Shouters Prohibition Ordinance of 1917, were generally presented in the calypsos of the 1930s as indulging in laughable or exotic rituals. In other words, the grass roots absorbed and disseminated comic caricatures of their own image, which they had derived from the country's ruling elite. There were, of course, a few exceptions, such as the Growling Tiger who in 'Yoruba Shango' acknowledges the power of the Orisha and the rooted strength of the tradition. But even Tiger, an extraordinarily conscious calypsonian who accurately defined the race and class situations of his time in compositions such as 'Workers' Appeal' (1935), 'Money is King' (1935), 'The Gold' (1936) and 'Let the White People Fight' (1942), derided the Baptists in 'What is the Shouter?' (1939).

> We have Roman Catholic, Anglican and Salvation
> But what is the Shouter band?
> If it is a religion do tell me please
> I am tired with the nonsense: give me an ease.
> The unknown twang on River Jordan
> Is the thing I can't understand.

The Shouters are viewed as devil-worshippers, 'With candle and a cross and a cycle bell/Invoking Lucifer in hell,' and ultimately as 'a disgrace to my native land.' Not surprisingly, Tiger applauds, as Louise Bennett's folk persona in 'Pinnacle' was to do in the early 1940s, the Police action in brutalising the Shouters (Rastafari in the case of 'Pinnacle').

> I read at Mount Hope the other day
> They had to chase some Shouter away
> With their head tie in white, with some long night gown
> While the police had them surround.
> In the height of the feast they began to moan
> Five mile apart you could hear them groan.
> A fellow said he came from Carriacou
> They burst his head with police butoo.[11]

Here we also have an intolerance of the migrant from Grenada, Carriacou, St Vincent and 'dem small islands.' The Shouters, a part of Trinidad for decades, are still being viewed as the purveyors of an alien religion, a style of worship vastly different from that of the respectable 'civilised' – Tiger uses the word in the calypso – 'Anglicans and Catholics'. Governor Sir John Chancellor and his 1917 law had done their job well. Propaganda against non European styles and customs had permeated the society at every level, so that the keepers of the tradition were themselves ambivalent about its deepest aspects, and could deal with it only on certain superficial planes. Even the recognized spokesmen of the people, calypsonians, when describing folk religions often assumed the essentially bourgeois role of the frightened or fascinated interloper describing quaintly excessive behaviour.

If the folk themselves had learned ambivalence, the natural reaction of the educated was to abandon folklore, folk music and religions and, seeking nineteenth century versions of the sublime, turn their poetry away from the sounds that were most familiar and the rhythms that were most available. Hence the disconnection between poetry and the oral tradition, poetry and the indigenous folk self. The growing nationalism during the 1930s and 40s resulted in attempts throughout the Antilles to rehabilitate the idea of the 'folk', and each territory possessed its people who were in the forefront of the movement to document and make visible the beleaguered culture of the people. Hence the importance of people such as Louise Bennett, Ivy Baxter, Lennox Pierre, Beryl McBurnie, Edric Connor, Olive Walke, and later, Wordsworth McAndrew, Jacob Elder, Rex Nettleford, Olive Lewin and Errol Hill. Along with the work of these West Indians was that of anthropologists such as Melville and Frances Herskovits, George Eaton Simpson, Daniel Crowley and Roger Abrahams. Their efforts ensured that the West Indies approached Independence with a much clearer notion of the breadth and potential of their folk and oral heritage.

There was in this rediscovery the inevitable question of how to accord the folk tradition an everyday normalcy and wholeness, when for so long it had been regarded as both esoteric and eccentric. The problem was whether a genuine folk heritage was still available for anything except anthropological enquiry. Mulattoes of culture who had had doubts before restated them now. Anthropological findings, according to Derek Walcott,[12] were signs that the folkways had become fakeways, and the order which anthropologists placed on the remnants of folk behaviour was abstract and unreal. Poets should be careful to avoid the 'pastoral' simplicity of an idealised and abstract folk world lest it lure them away from their real task of 'naming', without nostalgia, a unique new world, whose ancestral roots had become inaccessible, unnecessary and irrelevant. It wasn't that Walcott had not himself once believed that he could and should undertake:

> . . . the forging of a language that went beyond mimicry, a
> dialect which had the force of revelation as it invented
> names for things, one which finally settled on its own mode
> of inflection, and which began to create an oral culture of
> chants, jokes, folksongs and fables[13]

but that he believed everyone else's attempt to do the same was
spurious.

He also noted how after Independence, folk culture had been
exploited politically by both the local bourgeoisie and their fake-
radical opponents of Black Nationalist persuasion. It had thus
become the basis of both a thinly strident cultural nationalism
and a burgeoning tourist trade. There was now a fake folk
tradition which was removed from real life and that was its
greatest attraction.

Walcott's major criticism was that in writing 'immediate'
poetry, the poet does not listen to his 'inner ear'. He is conscious
of an audience, and produces a sort of easily communicable
theatre, which for all the immediacy of its relevance 'leaves out
the most exciting part of poetry, which is its craft.'[14] Walcott
admitted that the new poets were 'trying to reach closer to the
roots rhythms of the speech', but felt that they knew little about
crafting the poem. He contrasted the oral poets with poets such
as Dennis Scott, Anthony McNeill and Wayne Brown.

> Now if you look at the better poets of the younger genera-
> tion, there are three particular poets who are very fine and
> permanent poets. That's Wayne Brown, Anthony McNeill
> and Dennis Scott. They have the same power of impulse that
> the young polemic-type poets have. Their feelings are the
> same; they have the same bitterness, the same anger, the
> same drive. But when you read these poets, they are not
> using a language which is a platform language that can be
> delivered over to a waiting public. The intensity of their
> feeling is making their anguish extremely complex. In these
> poets, the language that is being used is not the 'down with
> the honky', a language of the people who consider them-
> selves to be the revolutionary poets.

> They are not using a platform language because the revolu-
> tion is being enacted inside of them. You mustn't trust
> revolutionary poets who can do a poem on a typewriter or a
> drum quickly, because when the Government changes,
> they'll turn out another one just as fast for you. You know.

It's no sweat. It's like editorial policy. Tomorrow it may change.[15]

In this interview, Walcott makes his usual clean distinction between the theatrical and the poetic; one which he had made earlier between the public nature of the calypso and the private nature of poetry, and which he'd maintained between his roles as poet and playwright. The problem with such a clean distinction when applied to West Indian poetry, is that it conceals the dialectical relationship between what Walcott presents as two opposite and irreconcilable poles. It also fails to recognize that a poetry based on the oral tradition would require, seek and create its own crafting. What the oral tradition demanded, then, was an alternative notion of crafting, one that Walcott needed to resist because it ran counter to the models he had studied.

(iv)

The lives of post-Independence proletarian youth were even grimmer than those of their newly uprooted peasant forebears. They faced in Jamaica a political reality of grim factional encounter between new alignments of the agricultural, commercial and intellectual elites scrambling to control a neglected peasantry and their migrant cousins, the urban dispossessed. Out of this tussle emerged the twin tendencies of reward via political patronage and bitter unrest among ordinary people, which led to creativity in music and verse as a means of coping with, understanding, giving utterance to and even celebrating the violence of their world. The tragic immediacy of this violence and the interplay of their own folk-urban culture with that of the similarly marginalised cultures of Afro-America and Black Britain, together fused to engender the culture of the youth, which in the 1970s spread throughout the Antilles and beyond.

The State throughout the West Indies was caught between impulses to market 'dread beat and blood' and to censor its subversive nature. Hence in Jamaica and Trinidad, the really penetrating political song has tended to receive little or no air play on the State-owned media. In spite of such stricture, a number of reggae singers, Dub poets and political calypsonians have emerged determined to speak from within the ghetto reality of their world. These are hardly voices that the State, concerned with appeasement, the tourist trade and the dollar, could afford to foster.

Thus Malik (Decoteau), Lasana Kwesi, Wayne Davis, Syl Lowhar and Lester Efebo Wilkinson were all political detainees in 1970 Trinidad. Leroy Calliste, a gentle poet, hanged himself. Wrongfully imprisoned, Jack Kelshall, an old time Marxist, wrote poems from prison. The disillusioned Eric Roach looked hard at the ghetto, wrote a score of post 1970 poems which contained a fierce clean bitterness, drank poison. Oku Onuora served several years in a Jamaican jail. Don Drummond, the shape of whose hurt inspired Anthony McNeill, died in the madhouse to which he had been committed for wife murder. Harold Simmons slashed his wrists and bled to death. Mikey Smith was stoned to death. Walter Rodney, not hearing or heeding the warning poem which Wordsworth McAndrew had addressed to him since 1976, in which he implored Rodney to leave a land which could find no use for his academic skills, became the occasion for further poetry when he was blown into fragments on June 13, 1980. McAndrew himself, Guyana's best folklorist and an accomplished radio personality, was forced to leave Guyana, because his superiors hated his style of dress and his forthrightness of speech. The manager of the warehouse where he first found work in New Jersey was amazed that a black could do simple arithmetic. 'Gee! He got them *all* right!'

What the State did with great efficiency was to promote Carnivals and festivals throughout the region. The most significant of these from the point of view of the Arts, has been *Carifesta*, which was sponsored in Guyana in 1972, and has since occurred in Jamaica, Cuba and Barbados. State policy, despite its obvious political pragmatism and its habitual brutality, has been beneficial to both folk and oral traditions, raising to the surface what had in the colonial era been submerged. Today, the oral tradition is alive both in its decorative aspects and as the vehicle of the passion of urban youth, concerned with creating shapes out of the grim immediacy of their situation.

(v)

The new wave of writers is not as easily divisible into distinct categories as Walcott has supposed. They have approached their heritage with a freedom rarely found in the pre-Independence era, seeking all available metaphors, sounds, rhythms and levels of sound and prosody. The Either/Or approach of the colonial era which had promoted English styled poetry and put down Caribbean orality was gradually replaced by the Both/And approach in which, as the situation demanded, writers varied freely along the continua between Folk and Modernist, Creole

11

and Standard, Oral and Scribal; the poem as uncurling tendril reaching out towards the Other, or self-sufficient pebble, total in the opacity of its own waterless universe; the poem as unfoldng chrysalis or transparent hard inert crystal. The mixture of qualities which Walcott sees in Scott, Brown and McNeill are in fact to be found in Brathwaite, Questel, Malik, Goodison, Philip and Mordecai. Walcott himself has yielded consistently to the pressure of the voice, his later work including several instances of the same orality that he had criticised in other poets. Perhaps the difference lies in the crafting.

Voiceprint is meant to illustrate not only the wealth and range of the West Indian oral tradition, but also the relationship between this tradition and a large body of writing which contains a certain orality even though this may not be immediately evident. It is important at this point to distinguish between folk and oral traditions. Though the folk tradition of the West Indies and perhaps of most places is largely oral, the oral tradition contains both folk working class and middle class elements; both 'black' and 'white' aspects of style. The sermon of the Anglican and Catholic or other establishment churches, is as much part of Caribbean oral tradition as Baptist shouting, Zion Revival 'trumping' or Rastafarian 'reasoning'. Calypsonians of the Oratorical period (1900–1920), listened to the orations of lawyers and bishops, according to Atilla the Hun. High-flown Tea Meeting speeches are as much part of traditional style as sharp grass-rooted 'tracings', or the clean razors of picong. The important link between each element is that of *voice*. The poems chosen here all contain voices. Voices signal the constant presence and pressure of people living immediate, unabstracted lives. So while our poets have at times expressed an admiration for such well known modernist trends as dryness, hardness, hermeticism or a monadic aestheticism in which poem, novel or play becomes a closed, self-contained system, there isn't one who hasn't responded to the immediacy of *people*.

(vi)

Our first oral category, *Legend, Tale, Narrative and Folk-Song*, includes both pre and post-Independence examples of how these forms have influenced the shape of West Indian poetry. Seymour's 'The Legend of Kaieteur' is an obvious example of legend. It tries for a speaking voice, employs dialogue at points and has a clear storyline. McAndrew's 'To a Carrion Crow' contrasts nicely with his celebrated 'Ol' Higue'. While both are dramatic addresses to an unanswering Other, 'To a Carrion Crow' is free verse and employs devices such as internal rhyming and metaphor. It not only invents a legend of the crow, but hints at an interpretation, the poet seeking meaning behind the plot's metaphor, in much the same way as the crow in hubris and wonder seeks meaning behind and beyond the sky's empty curvature. 'Ol' Higue', transcending earlier excursions into the vernacular such as the efforts of McTurk, is the first significant Guyana Creole poem. Addressing the 'Ol' woman wid de wrinkled skin', McAndrew recreates the legend of the Ol' Higue. Dramatic and incantatory after the style of *Macbeth*, it however breaks its lines and rhythms towards the end. Together, the two poems illustrate the point about poets who are comfortable at both poles of the continuum.

Narrative becomes increasingly more complicated in both plot and structure as one approaches contemporary times. Important landmarks in the progression of story telling in West Indian verse were Scott's 'Uncle Time' and Walcott's fine voice portraits, 'Tales of the Islands'. 'Uncle Time' obeys the allegorical impulse of the folk-tale, and employs not only a folk voice as narrator, but recognisable folk-tale characters and situations – the warmly avuncular but dirty and sinister old man, whose sexual play means blight, poison, bitterness and the withering of love; the legendary sly mongoose of one of the best known West Indian folk-songs, and most familiar of all, the deceitful anti-hero Anansi, who in folk tales is a blend of libido, trickery and intelligence. Like Anansi, Time is capable of rapid metamorphosis, from apparent and beguiling stasis to sudden and swift movement; from old man to sea-wind, to hill, to mongoose, to spider whose functions also change from love play to poisonous separating gossip, to ensnarement and finally, death-touch. The poem's major achievement is to have said all this in a folk Creole voice which changes fluidly in pace and tone as Time changes his masks.

In Chapter VI of 'Tales of the Islands': 'Poopa, da' was a fête', there is disjuncture between the seamless fluid connectedness of the line which doesn't 'let a comma in edgewise' and the disconnectedness of the information contained in the line. This disconnectedness is the poem's real subject matter; the separation between the jump and jive and the anguish it conceals; between awareness of pain, horror and tragedy and the attempt to drown it out by means of drunken stupor; the recognition of the vital subterranean presence of a folk tradition, and the recoil from its more negative and frightening aspect.

13

This disconnectedness will recur later in Victor Questel's 'Down Beat', where the moral emptiness of the street limer is expressed in terms of the equality of importance which he accords to cricket scores, rape, his sweet mas', pan music and prison. Questel's impulse here is essentially comic. The pun, the joke, are the corner-stones of his art. But even here the joke is close to the possibility of madness. By 'Pan Drama', in the category *Pan, Calypso, and Rapso Poems*, the narrative voice has already withdrawn into its loneliness. The persona there, as in Paul Keens-Douglas's 'Jus' Like Dat' is commenting on the masquerade after Carnival. Keens-Douglas's voice is that of a reveller awakening stale-drunk on the pavement on Ash Wednesday morning, wondering how he got there, and piecing together his haphazard drift 'jus' like dat' from vacancy through masquerade to dereliction and vagrancy. His story is the country's central fable and journey to which its poets and novelists and calypsonians continually return. Its major myth is the passage from mas' to mass, or 'steered between, ole mas and half-mast' as Questel puts it in his variation of the national pun.

The narrator of Questel's 'Pan Drama', like that of Walcott's 'Mass Man', has never been a participant: and thus has not even the memory of fantasy to sustain his reverie. The pan man, 'attuned to the base tenor' of his daily ghetto existence becomes the poet's double, because of his skill at creating harmony and attunement out of the unrelated fragments of existence. It is interesting to listen to the calypsonian Relator work in 'Deaf Pan Men' with the same image of the pan man. Only here, the deafness of the pan man is related to that of the country's political leader, while the disharmony which ensues from the pan man's deafness is related to a fragmented society in which everyone is going in his own individual direction. Calypso too had moved towards metaphor over the years of its emergence from the kalinda and bel air.

Questel as a poet generally works with unrelated images, the odds and ends of experience. This tendency is fuelled by, as it strives to explore, a fear of cracks within the psyche, an awareness of madness, blankness, void, the black hole of breakdown. His poems and plays display the two sides of Trinidad's famous schizophrenia, not as separate halves, but intermixed so that in one half – the gaiety, the brilliance and the laughter – lies the ever imminent possibility of the other – the break-up, the breakdown. Hence his commitment to the pun, not only as irritating ornament but as driven necessity. For in the pun lies the doubleness of vision, the duplicity of meaning and possibility which he sees in life, as well as the means of transcending the despair of the condition. 'Hitting the bottle, my faith splinters.'

The fragmented narrative is taken to even more desperate extremes by Mikey Smith in 'Me Cyaan Believe It', and Jean Binta Breeze's 'Riddym Ravings', both of which present kaleidoscopes of the city's derangement. Smith shapes narrative fragments into sharply dislocated and rapidly changing impressions of voice and image. In a sense, the narrator is similar to that of Questel's 'Down Beat', save for the menacing grimness of what is recalled: the struggle for existence alongside 'cockroach rat an scorpion,' Anansi 'politricks' in which the 'yout' are pitted against each other in sacrificial waste; prostitution, recurrent pregnancy; the casual pointlessness of violent encounter on the streets; that horrible Orange Lane fire in which children and mothers were fed to flames by gunmen. That incident recurs as tragic nightmare in recent Jamaica poems (e.g. Scott's 'Dreadwalk', Brathwaite's 'Poem for Walter Rodney', Hippolyte's 'Orange Lane: The Fire's Light'). It climaxes the list of incredible events and images which provide Smith's narrator with his now famous refrain 'Me cyaan believe it'.

Jean Binta Breeze's mad woman represents a further development of the fragmented fable. She's Slade Hopkinson's 'Madwoman of Papine', Roger McTair's deranged prophetess of 'Ganja Lady', the mother who 'gleams from the ghetto' in Brathwaite's 'Springblade', and who will throw the first stone to which even now her claws of fingers are irreversibly hooked. The difference between the voice-portrait and the monologue/ narrative is that in the latter the voice speaks from *within* the experience. 'The Madwoman of Papine', Walcott's 'Laventille' and McTair's 'Ganja Lady' are voice-portraits. The voice describes a situation which is clearly seen from outside. Malik's two 'Pan Run' poems, Mikey Smith's 'Me Cyaan Believe It', Questel's 'Down Beat' and 'Pan Drama', Binta Breeze's 'Riddym Ravings' and Mutabaruka's 'A Sit Dung Pon de Wall' are monologues which take us inside the minds of the narrators.

Binta Breeze's madwoman is telling the story of her derangement. It begins with her movement to the alienating city, continues with her eviction and subsequent vagrancy, and climaxes with her obsession that within her head there's a radio with a DJ constantly playing a reggae refrain:

Eh eh
No feel no way
Town is a place dat a really kean stay

Dem kudda – ribbit mi han
Eh – ribbit mi toe
Mi waan go a country go look mango.

But the healing journey back to country, to land, ground, family, community and endless fruit – which is a recurring theme in Jamaican literature, from Mais's *The Hills Were Joyful Together*, and 'All Men Come to the Hills Finally', through Barrett's *Song for Mumu*, Brodber's *Jane and Louisa* and Senior's *Talking of Trees*, especially 'Reaching My Station', and *Summer Lightning* – never occurs. The cleansing bath which she (the madwoman) attempts one day at a city sidewalk standpipe is interpreted as a further sign of madness and she's taken to the madhouse where the doctor and the landlord, the two evil geniuses of her world, try to remove the radio from her head. This obsessive sound, her song and lament, is at once the sign of her derangement and her last point of connection with her first world and her story. So pregnant, abused, but existing in a strangely happy space within her cracked head, she clings to the lifeline of her radio, her story, her refrain, tricking the doctor and the landlord by reconnecting whenever they disconnect her from her dream.

Other extended narratives include Pamela Mordecai's 'Southern Cross' and James Berry's 'Chain of Days.' These are, however, more connected – as the metaphor of a chain of days suggests. The narrators here have an autobiographical sanity, a nostalgic security based on their memories of rural childhood, Binta Breeze's narrator, by contrast, lives for a past she'll never regain, but which she has made her only reality, negating the urban experience.

Binta Breeze's 'Riddym Ravings' recalls Shadow's calypso 'Bass Man', where the narrator is plagued by a monstrous double named Farrell, who controls his creative impulse by constantly pulling the strings of his bass. The Bass Man is his muse, the source of the driving, new, hypnotic rhythm which Shadow brought to the calypso in 1971. But the Bass Man is also a fixed obsession, a demon of rhythm, the monstrous double of imagination of which Shadow seeks to unburden himself, the Other whom he feels an urge to kill; Shadow's Shadow. The 'Bass Man' electrified Trinidad in 1974. 'Shadowmania' became a new Trinidad word by 1975, as the society recognized its dark double of creative obsessional energy in the earth of Shadow's harsh-sweet tones.

(vii)

The elegy has become a predominant mode in West Indian poetry, perhaps because St John Perse's 'tristes tristes tropiques' still produce much that can evoke lamentation. Here the elegies in the category *Elegy, Lament* are for the society itself, or for its many failures and victims. These laments explore every register along the speech continuum, and include Linton Kwesi Johnson's beautiful 'Reggae for Radni'.

Other laments are for the general state of things, (e.g. Eric Roach's 'Hard Drought'), for the failure of some great moment (Salkey's 'Maurice', Johnson's 'Reggae for Radni'). Roger McTair's 'March February Remembering', included for its cool dreaming narrative voice in the first section, also belongs here. These categories are not meant to be exclusive; many poems belong to several of them. Many of these elegies are also praise songs, which seek to celebrate the qualities of the person who has died. This is particularly true of those which are dedicated to artists, poets and musicians. Harold Simmons becomes for Walcott 'the fervour and intelligence of an entire island', Drummond becomes for McNeill his guide through dread city and the dark places of the heart.

(viii)

The Dub poems of the category *Dread Talk, Dub, Sermon, Prophesight and Prophesay* are poems which have grown directly out of the speech and music rhythms of reggae and Rastafari. They represent an extension of the much older toaster tradition, which in Jamaica involved the DJ talking smart, slick and often silly jingles into the microphone, either in introduction of a tune or in the spaces between the music. This was happening with Ska in the early sixties, and developed further with Rock Steady, a music with wider spaces.

Technological change in the mixing of music, the advent of the 16-track tape and easy over-dubbing, the development of the synthesiser, intensified the DJ's role as manipulator of sound, juggler of gimmicks, controller of rhythm and pace, exhorter of the audience, who would be soldiered into jumping, prancing, raising their hands in the air, wining, grinding, and jamming, getting up or getting down to it. The DJ became high priest in the cathedral of canned sound, fragmented discotheque image projections, broken lights, and youth seeking lost rituals amid the smoke of amnesia.

17

Dub poetry is at its worst a kind of tedious jabber to a monotonous rhythm. At its best it is the intelligent appropriation of the manipulatory techniques of the DJ for purposes of personal and communal signification. As I said earlier, the Dub poet speaks from *within* the ghetto experience, clarifying the battle between uprooted youth and the entrenched social system. Of all the poems included here, the Dub poem needs most to be heard, and there are excellent recordings of Linton Kwesi Johnson, Oku Onuora, Michael Smith, Binta Breeze and Mutabaruka. Space does not permit a full discussion of these poets in performance. The very nature of reggae, heavy bass-line and space between voice and 'riddim' with horns or synthesiser muted in the middle range, generally means that one can hear every word of the performance. Sound is stripped down to the skeleton of riddim, with the superimposition of the flesh of voice in performance. In Dub one scarcely runs the risk of the voice having to compete against its accompaniment as frequently happens with calypso in performance.

One danger that does exist though, is to believe that riddim can or should be allowed to become the sole foundation of the dub poem's appeal. The better poets avoid this pitfall, first of all by making subtle variations in tone, pace and the heaviness of the beat. The heavier the beat, the more 'dread' the emotion. There is a whole vocabulary of tone and feeling contained in what Linton Kwesi Johnson has identified as 'bass culture'. Apart from variation in how a regular bass-line is employed, there is the technique of breaking up the poem, so that it varies between unaccompanied monologue and those sequences where the voice follows the contour of the beat. In 'Reggae for Dada', Linton Kwesi Johnson employs this technique in order to vary mood of the poem between sorrow for his father, relief at his release from Jamaican life and bitterness at the fact that the country could have offered no more than this mean, unchanging bareness.

Sometimes the poem is for unaccompanied voice. This type of poem usually allows the performer greater freedom, since the bass-line no longer controls its movement. The unaccompanied voice is particularly effective in Mutabaruka's 'Sit Dung Pon De Wall', whose theme is precisely that of the menacing silence which exists between the terrified passer-by and the vagrant, society and its double. The poem has a freedom of voice, and contains a certain humour of the grotesque, oddly similar to that of Kendel Hippolyte's 'Zoo Story'.[16] In both cases, the deadpan tone of the narrating voice conceals the horror of what is being narrated, a tragic and unnecessary accident in the case of

18

Mutabaruka; the fatal encounter between dungle dread and jungle lion in the zoo's symbolic space, in the case of Hippolyte. Binta Breeze's performance of 'Riddym Ravings' also employs the relative silence of the unaccompanied voice to convey the rational irrationality of a woman who, pushed beyond the threshold of pain, no longer feels anything. Here too there is the mixture of humour and horror, as the madwoman sanely talks about the radio inside her head.

The narrator of Mutabaruka's 'Sit Dung Pon De Wall' is a street dweller whose only connection with the well-dressed, faint-hearted passer-by is through the silent exchange of glances which are neutral on the part of the narrator, wary on the part of the passer-by. As soon as the vagrant changes his normal position the self-affrighted passer-by panics, runs into the path of a passing car and is killed. A menacing, tantalizing poem, it provokes thought as to its hidden meaning.

Oku consciously tries for a menacing tone in poems such as 'Pressure Drop'. His style blends chant and statement, with the guttural voice expressing at times a great sadness, at others a great indignation. There is sincerity and fervour in the voice as the poet tries to transcend the written word and become himself the poem. Oku defines this ordeal precisely when he declares:

        I am no poet
                no poet
        I am just a voice.
        I echo the people's
                thought
                laughter
                cry
                sigh. . .
        I am no poet
                no poet

        I am just a voice

The aim of the Dub poet, then, is to *submerge identity in voice*. This does not mean, however, that these poets really abandon their individuality. Mikey Smith's performances are absolutely individual. His use of voice, his honing of voice to stark sheer scrape of sound; his prolonged 'Lawwwwwwwwwwwwd' cannot be imitated. Of the Dub poets, he was probably the most flexible, the one who had the greatest impulse to abandon the beat and allow the voice to establish its own rhythm.

Dub poetry, and indeed, much of the poetry of the oral tradition, employs repetition as an essential technique. Malik's elegy for Mikey Smith, 'Instant Ting' employs a technique found in some folk ballads, where each stanza advances the plot by one idea, inching it towards its climax. Mikey is simultaneously recognized by both his admirers and his enemies. His admirers recognize him as a hero: 'swift as ah hawk /With ah hop an drop walk'. His enemies instantaneously recognize him as target for the stone. It is as if he draws their menace upon himself, by his too visible and defiant independence of spirit. The poem limps on its hop and drop Legba rhythm towards the menace of the stone, its muttering bass varying by semi-tones.

(ix)

Dub poems are heavy with testimony, warning and prophecy. So too are many post 1970 calypsoes, a few of which have even incorporated reggae rhythms and dread themes. The calypsoes selected here (under the category *Calypso*) illustrate a range of themes, concerns and styles. The eloquence and wonder in the word inherited from the Oratorical period are clearly seen in Atilla's 'Graf Zeppelin'. Tiger's 'The Gold' helped arouse public opinion in Trinidad during the Italian invasion of Abyssinia. The strong narrative quality and the often bizarre humour of the calypso are illustrated in Kitchener's 'Take Your Meat Out Me Rice' and Spoiler's 'Fountain of Youth'. Protest, complaint, satire and wisdom may be seen in this anthology in the calypsoes of Relator, Sparrow and Valentino.

Always strong in sexual metaphor, calypsoes gradually expanded their metaphorical range, and in the period after 1970 began to reveal an admirable control of image and idea. Penguin's 'The Devil' (1980) redefines evil in secular and political terms, employing the vocabulary and rhythm of the old-time devil band. This is a calypso which develops a single image, providing several illustrations of the devil theme, throughout its length. It ends with an ironic twist typical of the decade when it warns the society:

> And if you praise the wrongs men do
> Well then you is a devil too.

Society is diabolical because it has permitted the devil to exist.

Calypsonians, after a decade of assigning blame to politicians for the ills of society, had begun to turn their scrutiny upon the nation itself. Even Valentino, dubbed 'the people's calypsonian' after 1970 because of the sincerity and plaintive strength of his songs, blames the people at large in Trinidad in his magnificent 'Dis Place Nice'.

Here, the coherence of the calypso depends on a constant exposure of the old calypso cliche 'Trinidad is nice/Trinidad is a paradise'. This cliche has become one of the stockphrases of the patriotic calypso, and it had become fashionable in post 1970 calypsoes to comment ironically on rooted attitudes and catch-phrases. Mighty Chalkdust, for example, rejected the 'smutty calypso' in 'Why Smut' and 'Juba Dubai'. Stalin turned Sniper's 'Portrait of Trinidad' inside out with his 'New Portrait to Trinidad'.

The calypsonian has emerged, then, as a critic of conscious-ness, and the calypso has become aware of itself, its formal potentialities and limitations, its confused and everchanging position. This suggests that the calypsonian has begun the journey towards an inclusion of the full range of human emo-tions in what used to be a form where only certain types of feeling or mood such as celebration, praise, censure, erotic desire, ridicule were admitted. Stalin's 'Make Them All Right' (1984) approached anguish and compassion, while Delamo's apocalyptic condemnation of human limitation in 'Sodom and Gomorrah' (1982) and 'Armageddon' (1984) is, if hopeless, still a genuinely anguished cry from the heart.

The calypso captures a delicate balance between the plainest and the most metaphorical speech. Drawing instinctively on the religious base, it yet understands that it must secularise myth if myth is to make any sense in an agnostic age. The growing dimension of the calypso inspired Derek Walcott to attempt a long satirical and narrative poem in a simplified version of the calypso rhythm. In this poem, 'The Spoiler's Return' (in the category *Pan, Calypso and Rapso Poems*), the ghost of one of the most famous calypsonians of the 50s returns from hell to denounce Trinidad for its myriad failures. The Spoiler functions as persona for Walcott himself, and the poem, like 'The Schoon-er *Flight*' is meant not only to lacerate, but to justify the poet's belated self-exile from a country which had always evoked in him feelings of helplessness and rage.

Also worthy of note in the section *Pan, Calypso, and Rapso Poems* are the Rapso poems of Brother Resistance. A development of the 'talk-songs' (my term) of Trinidad musician Lancelot Layne, Jamaican Dub, calypso and Afro-American rapping songs, the

Rapso themes are essentially those we've already discussed in the section on Dub: blackness, poverty, ghetto culture, vagrancy, Africa, 'the struggle', Apartheid. Like Dub it is a performed art, but it is still a new and undeveloped form. Brother Resistance, a UWI graduate, represents a new type: that of the grass roots intellectual for whom the very world and word of the intellectual is an abstraction that needs to be resisted, lest it direct vision away from the immediacy of social reality. Just as Walcott instinctively resists the pressure of the oral tradition, making concessions to it only when it has through its own efforts gained in depth and dimension, Brother Resistance struggles against the treacherous voids which underlie the world of 'Book' ('Book so Deep'), measuring as did Lamming's G, the price which he had paid in being educated beyond his reality.

The Pan poems, which have their counterpart in a large number of calypsoes about the steel band, usually derive their metaphors from the steelband, whose rhythms they may try to imitate. The most significant of these are Malik's monologues, 'Pan Run I' and 'Pan Run II'[17] and John Agard's 'Man to Pan'. Agard's 'Man to Pan' pays homage to its predecessors, the poems of Brathwaite, Malik, Kitchener and Keens-Douglas, and is a sustained experiment with shape, rhythm and metaphor. Its climax is a roadmarch, whose narrator is Spree Simon, one of the fathers of Pan.

(x)

The other poems included in *Voiceprint* fall into familiar categories. As in the other categories, a wide range of linguistic registers is represented. *Signifying: Robbertalk* is a term borrowed from Afro-American streetlore to describe the tendency of black men towards heroic self-identification. This tendency was also strong in the West Indies, and once formed the core of the Oratorical or Sans Humanite tradition in the calypso. In this collection, the term is applied to poems of self-identification, particularly those that locate the individual in the political or historical moment. Not all of these, however, are expressions of heroic self-confidence. There are also many poems which express a brooding self-doubt or a qualified pessimism.

Praise songs, prayers and incantations are also included. These are the opposite of tracings, curses and warnings, for which the islands are renowned, and which are well represented here. Political manifestos and satirical pieces are also included. *Word-Songs* constitute an unusual category; but it was felt that this considerable body of poems about music, or poems which capture the lilt of song should be represented here. Even here there is voice. Collymore's 'Hymn to the Sea' is a kind of monologue, as is Roach's 'Transition' and Goodison's 'Mulatta Song'. McNeill addresses his ecstatic music poems to the unanswering void that he terms 'Ungod', Christine Craig to a saxophone player. Several other poems located in other categories might fit here.

Taken together, the poems in this collection illustrate that a West Indian aesthetic will embrace all ways of saying, all language registers, however different some of these may seem or be; that each type of saying requires its particular skill for shaping voice; that 'Man must chant as man can gainst night.'[18]

Footnotes

1 G. Rohlehr, 'The Problem of the Problem of Form: The idea of an aesthetic continuum and aesthetic code-switching in West Indian Literature.' *Anales del Caribe*, 6, 1986, pp.218-277, Havana, Casa de las Americas

2 G. Rohlehr, *Pathfinder: Black Awakening in 'The Arrivants' of Edward Kamau Brathwaite*, Trinidad, 1981, (self published)

3 See Brathwaite's *Contradictory Omens*, UWI, Mona, Jamaica, 1974, for the term 'inter-creolization'

4 Joe Harriott, Johnny Mayer et al., *Fusions*, EMI Records, SX6122 & *Indo-Jazz Suite*, Atlantic, SD 1465

5 A. Jarvis, *Bamboula Drum*, St Thomas, V.I., The Art Shop, 1935, in Krauz Reprint, Germany, 1970

6 P. Curtin, *The Image of Africa: British Ideas and Action, 1780–1850*, Wisconsin, University of Wisconsin Press, 1964

7 G. Rohlehr, 'Calypso Censorship: Historical' in *Seminar on the Calypso*, UWI, Trinidad, ISER, 1986

8 E. Roach, *Trinidad Guardian*, 14 Jan. 1971 see also Rohlehr, G., 'Some Problems of Assessment', *Caribbean Quarterly*, Vol. 17 Nos. 3 & 4 (Sept–Dec. 1971) pp. 92–113

9 *ibid*

10 See E. Lovelace, *The Wine of Astonishment*, London, Deutsch, 1982

11 N. Marcano (The Growling Tiger) 'What is the Shouter?', New York, Decca, 1939 (This extract taken from unpublished version in Government Archives of Trinidad and Tobago.)

12 D. Walcott, 'What the Twilight Says: An Overture,' in *Dream on Monkey Mountain and Other Plays*, New York, Farrar, Strauss & Giroux, 1970

13 *ibid*, p. 17

14 D. Walcott, Interviewed by Raoul Pantin in *Caribbean Contact*, Vol. 1, No. 7, July 1973, pp. 14–16 & Vol. 1, No. 8, August 1973, pp. 14–16 Quotation from Part 2, August 1973, p. 14

15 *ibid*

16 G. Rohlehr, 'The Problem of the Problem of Form'. Hippolyte's 'Zoo Story' discussed – see footnote 1

17 G. Rohlehr, 'My Strangled City', *Caliban* Vol 2, No. 1 Fall/Winter, 1976

18 D. Scott, 'More Poem' in *Dreadwalk*, London, New Beacon Books Ltd, 1982, p.3

Note: not all the poems quoted in the introduction are in *Voiceprint*. Refer to the indices at the back to check those included.

Legend, Tale, Narrative, and Folk-Song

The Legend of Kaieteur

Now Makonaima, the Great Spirit, dwelt
In the huge mountain rock that throbbed and felt
The swift black waters of Potaro's race
Pause on the lip, commit themselves to space
5   And dive the half mile to the rocks beneath.
Black were the rocks with sharp and angry teeth
And on those rocks the eager waters died,
Lost their black body, and up the mountain side,
Above the gorge that seethed and foamed and hissed
10 Rose, resurrected into lovely mist.

The rock He lived in towered a half mile high
So that it seemed a rival to the sky
And over it this living mist He drew
To curtain off Divinity from view.
15 He gave it too the privilege to choose
To take the glory of the rainbow's hues
To wear at morning, and for changed delight
The marvellous sunsets of the tropic night.
From day to day, behind this rainbowed screen,
20 The Father, the inscrutable, unseen,
Would ponder on His domain of the earth
And all the nations He had given birth.

And He caused flowers to weave upon the ground
Their rich embroideries, and He set around
25 The village where each tribe worked all day long
A veritable tapestry of song
From birds that in the branches built their bowers
And spent within the shade quick musical hours.
So every wind blew peace and fortune down
30 From the sweet heavens, and everywhere was sung
A song of praise to the Great Spirit above
That fathered them in kindliness and love.
And every moon each tribe would come and float

Upon the stream a sacrifical boat
35 New-carved and painted, laden with fish and fruit
And watch it gain speed as it neared and shoot
Over the rock into the gorge below.

And as the waters, so the centuries flow
Until the savage Caribishi came
40 And put the Patamoona to the flame.
They came by night and took them in their sleep
Slaughtered the guards and drove away the sheep
Ravished the women, burnt their huts and fields,
Despite their warclubs and their wooden shields.
45 A few, the merest remnant, took to flight
And under shelter of the friendly night
Escaped from the pursuing torches sent
To slay them in the caches where they went.
These took the terrible tidings of the raid
50 To the far camp their restless kin had made
On the Potaro – that the feud was awake
And counsel what defences they could make.

Old Kaie was chief in counsel. He was wise
Over a hundred seasons had those eyes
55 Seen in their passage. Time had made them dim
But with its wisdom compensated him.
He knew the cures for all men's ills and fears
And he had words for women in their tears
To comfort them. He sat all day and talked
60 Unto the tribe, for painfully he walked
On legs like rotten trunks wherein chigoes
Had nested and made caves of all his toes.
Just now he counselled, 'Since our arms are small
I and another to the mountain wall
65 Will go to question Makonaima's will
What he requires that we must fulfil
In sacrificial offerings. He is kind
His orders will chase fear out of our mind.'
Then someone murmured 'But can Kaie's feet stand
70 The troublesome journey through steep, rocky land?'
Flame sprang to Kaie's eyes, 'Will you never learn,
From what the mind wills, body will not turn?'

So the next morning laboured up the slope
Kaie and the one other with their ropes
75 Strapped round their backs, their bags of magic art
With all the stuff that in their spells had part.

Kaie's feet oft staggered and the westering sun
Was swallowed up by night, the day was done
Before they came upon the slab of stone
80 That ends the path to the Great Spirit's home.

                                                Alone

They stood while the vast starry night was full
Of falling water. Kaie felt his fellow pull
His arm. 'Look there', 'Yes, Makonaima's birds,
They are His messengers, they speak his words.
85 These small black cruiser birds, they fly in flocks
And feed on lana seed among the rocks.'
And now the birds made swoopings round the pair
And chattering, brushed Kaie's cheek and kissed his ear.
Twice, thrice, they did this. Then with sudden flight
90 They wheeled and veered off through the seeing Night.

Then in a voice that swelled and sank and broke
With the great wealth of joy he felt, Kaie spoke
'Oh, great is Makonaima and the words
That he has spoken by message of His birds
95 I must go down the passage of the river
That I may sit before His face for ever
In His great house, the everlasting rock.
And He has promised that no harm, no shock
Shall bruise our people, for His watch and ward
100 Shall circle us and He shall be our guard.

I am accounted for a sacrifice
For all the tribe. You with your younger eyes
Shall see the offering that you may tell
How boldly Kaie clasped such a death, how well
105 He lost his life to save his threatened race
And shadow them with the eternal peace.'

So in the morning, while the dim mist wreathed
And the fall thundered and the deep forge seethed
That other sat at vantage by the wall
110 And scanned the river to the waterfall.
He saw the sun o'er-peep the world and throw
Tide after tide of golden ray and glow
Against the fall, flood full on its attire,
Its misty veil, and catch that mist afire.
115 Amazed, he stared. The opalescent light
Deepened and sank and changed. . . .Then in his sight

Below the point that Kaie had bid him mark
He saw Kaie in a sacrificial bark.

120 The frail boat bobbed and bucked within the grip
Of the live waters that hurried it to the lip
Over the abyss. Kaie then raised his tall
Huge bulk in the boat and towered over the fall,
A cruciform over the flaming mist.
Then with a force that nothing could resist
125 The boat rent all that misty veil in two,
Drawing a dark line down the rainbow hue.

But of Kaie's body never showed a trace,
He sat with Makonaima before His face.

ARTHUR SEYMOUR
Guyana

Electric Eel Song

From a play. Gentle, almost inaudible steel pans.

Ay! me one child! Ay-eeee!
 Ay! me one daughter!
Take out you' foot
 From the black river water!
5 Haul back you' hand
 Out the slow river water!
Stay 'pon the bank
 Of the cold river water!
 Ay! me one daughter!
10   Ay! me one child! Ay-eeee!

Electric eel
 Is the eel in the river
Shadow 'pon the bottom
 Is the eel in the river
15 Something like you' hand
 Is the eel in the river
Swimming like you' foot
 Is the eel in the river

Ay! me one child! Ay-eeee!
20 Ay! me one daughter!

Foot after foot
    Through the black river water!
She can't touch the bottom
    Of the slow river water!
25 Skirt like umbrella
    In the cold river water!
    Ay! me one daughter!
        Ay! me one child! Ay-eeee!

Electric eel
30   Is the eel in the river
Cutlass shape
    Is the eel in the river
Black blade or brown
    Is the eel in the river
35 Dozing so quiet
    Is the eel in the river

Ay! me one child! Ay-eeee!
    Ay! me one daughter!
Slap of a tail
40   Through the black river water!
Shiver like ague
    In the slow river water!
As if she take cramp
    From the cold river water
    Ay! me one daughter!
        Ay! me one child! Ay-eeee!

Electric eel
    Is the eel in the river
No blood, just a thrill,
50   Is the eel in the river
Lightning bolt
    Is the eel in the river
And she drown now, she chilly
    Is the eel in the river

55 Ay! me one daughter!
Ay! me one child! Ay-eeee!

SLADE HOPKINSON
Guyana

To a Carrion Crow

They call you Carrion Crow
scorn to eat your flesh
spit when they see you administering the last rites
call you Cathartes: the Clean-up,
5 yet if they only knew the
secret of your strange religion.

Once you were the silver bird of the heavens
once you flew as high and as free
as only a bird can. The sky was yours
10 for you were king of the air
               but here
was the secret of your discontent:
it was not enough to just live and die,
not-knowing. You kept asking, whence came I,
15 whither go I, and why? The sky
must hold the answer, you thought,
and sought long and desperately
to glimpse what lay beyond it.

Relentlessly you fought
20 pitted bone and feather and tendon
against the blue barrier that mocked you, locked you off
from the secret world behind its curvature.
But you were more determined than it knew
             and could fly higher.
25 So you perspired at your quest
until one inspired day you flew
so hard and so fast against the blue
closing your wings at the last
minute for penetration
30 that at last you had a look at the other side.

Nobody knows what you saw
when you passed through
but you burned in that sacred blue fire
and returned, black as coals, dumb,
35 numb from the experience
to become this mendicant preacher
minister to those souls who die without sacrament
trading blessings for food
a saved soul for a full belly.
40 And now when I see you
crowding a carcass for the unction

or nailed against the sky like a crucifix
with the two spots of tarnished silver
beneath your wings when you'd closed them
45 I long to have you say a De Profundis for me
when I die, and I wonder:

Was yours a punishment or a purification?

WORDSWORTH McANDREW
Guyana

Ol' Higue

Ol' woman wid de wrinkled skin,
Leh de ol' higue wuk begin.
Put on you fiery disguise,
Ol' woman wid de weary eyes.
5   Shed you swizzly skin.

Ball o' fire, raise up high.
Raise up till you touch de sky.
Land 'pon top somebody roof.
Tr'ipse in through de keyhole – poof!
10   Open you ol' higue eye.

Find de baby where 'e lie.
Change back faster than de eye.
Find de baby, lif' de sheet,
Mek de puncture wid you teet',
15   Suck de baby dry.

Before 'e wake an' start to cry,
Change back fast, an' out you fly.
Find de goobie wid you skin.
Mek you semidodge, then – in!
20   Grin you ol' higue grin.

In you dutty-powder gown
Next day schoolchildren flock you round.
"Ol' higue, ol' higue!" dey hollerin out.
Tek it easy, hold you mout'.
25   Doan leh dem find you out.

Dey gwine mark up wid a chalk
Everywhere wheh you got to walk –
You bridge, you door, you jalousie –
But cross de marks an' leh dem see.
30   Else dey might spread de talk.

Next night you gone out jus' de same,
Wrap up in you ball o' flame,
To find an' suck another child.
But tikkay! Rumour spreadin' wild.
35   An' people know you name.

Fly across dis window-sill.
Why dis baby lyin' so still?
Lif' de sheet like how you does do.
Oh God! Dis baby nightgown blue!
40   Run fo' de window-sill!

Woman you gwine run or not?
Doan mind de rice near to de cot.
De smell o' asafoetida
Like um tek effect 'pon you.
45   You wan' get kyetch or what?

But now is too late for advice,
'Cause you done start to count de rice
An' if you only drop one grain
You must begin it all again.
50   But you gwine count in vain.

Whuh ah tell you?

Day done light an' rice still mountin'
Till dey wake an' kyetch you countin'
An' pick up de big fat cabbage broom
55 An' beat you all around de room.
                    Is now you should start countin'

Whaxen! Whaxen! Whaxen! Plai!
You gwine pay fo' you sins befo' you die.
Lash she all across she head.
60 You suck me me baby till um dead?
                    Whaxen! Whaxen! Plai!

You feel de manicole 'cross you hip?
Beat she till blood start to drip.
"Ow me God! You bruk me hip!
65 Done now, nuh? Allyou done!"

Is whuh you sayin' deh, you witch?
Done? Look, allyou beat de bitch.
Whaxen! Whaxen! Pladai! Plai!
Die, you witch you. Die!
70 Whaxen!
       Whaxen!
              Plai!

WORDSWORTH McANDREW
Guyana

Tales of the Islands
Chapter VI

Poopa, da' was a fête! I mean it had
Free rum free whisky and some fellars beating
Pan from one of them band in Trinidad
And everywhere you turn was people eating
5 And drinking and don't name me but I think
They catch his wife with two tests up the beach
While he drunk quoting Shelley with 'Each
Generation has its *angst*, but we has none'
And wouldn't let a comma in edgewise.
10 (Black writer chap, one of them Oxbridge guys.)
And it was round this part once that the heart
Of a young child was torn from it alive
By two practitioners of native art,
But that was long before this jump and jive.

DEREK WALCOTT
St Lucia

Uncle Time

Uncle Time is a ole, ole man. . . .
All year long 'im wash 'im foot in de sea,
long, lazy years on de wet san'
an' shake de coconut tree dem
5 quiet-like wid 'im sea-win' laughter,
scraping away de lan'. . .

Uncle Time is a spider-man, cunnin' an' cool,
him tell yu: watch de hill an' yu se mi.
Huhn! Fe yu yi no quick enough fe si
10 how' im move like mongoose; man, yu tink 'im fool?

32

Me Uncle Time smile black as sorrow;
'im voice is sof' as bamboo leaf
but Lawd, me Uncle cruel.
When 'im play in de street
15 wid yu woman – watch 'im! By tomorrow
she dry as cane-fire, bitter as cassava;
an' when 'im teach yu son, long after
yu walk wid stranger, an' yu bread is grief.
Watch how 'im spin web roun' ya house, an' creep
20 inside; an' when 'im touch yu, weep. . . .

DENNIS SCOTT
Jamaica

Roas' Turkey

Gal, run go wash de jesta-pot!
Ketch up de fire, Fred!
Tell Lou fi sen some seasonin –
Miss Marie turkey dead!

5 De turkey wake up hearty an
Was strollin bout de place
When him an Kate half-starvin dog
Just buck up face to face!

De turkey stop, de dog jaw drop,
10 Him lick him mout an work i,
Him meck a robot-bomber dive
An pounce dung pon de turkey!

Miss Marie bawl out, 'Save de turkey!'
'Kill de dog!' Po soul!
15 Two man run out fi help her, but
Dat time de turkey cole!

Po Marie dissa groan an sigh
An swear her heart stop beat,
She teck oat when de turkey cook
20 She hooden touch de meat!

Me mout start sympatize wid her
An tell her seh she right,
But hear me heart: 'Teng Gad! Fi-me
Belly gwine bus tenight!'

33

25 So run go beg Fan two stale bread!
Beg Jane some coaknut-ile!
Talk loud meck grudgeful Emma know
Seh we gwine eat in style!

Dem seh, 'When horse dead cow fat', an
30 'Puss laugh when pear-tree fall';
So me gwine full me belly, while
Miss Marie she dah bawl!

LOUISE BENNETT
Jamaica

Cousin Joe

Puppa, me go a Kingston an
Me meet up Cousin Joe
An ah start fi swell wid proudness
From me head to me big toe,
5 For not anodder man in tung
Is high like Cousin Joe.

Who him igh like? Me no know.
King no igh like Cousin Joe.
Sarjan Major? Puppa, cho!
10 Governor? Inspector? Poh!
Wey yuh seh? Prime Minister?
Higher, Puppa! Higher, sah!

Yuh naw listen to me, no?
Joe jus come outa depot!
15 Dat-deh place, it mussa gran!
For wid staff eena him han
Joe is tellin everybady 'Move awn!'

Puppa, him got awn boot a foot
An helmet pon him head
20 An him got awn stiff white jacket
An black trousiz trim wid red.
Ah never see nobady drested
So from ah was bawn.
Him jus walkin up an dung
25 Like him own de ole a tung
Just telling everybady 'Move awn!'

When de bus was leavin tung,
As we ketch whe four road meet
Me see Cousin Joe dah stan up
30 In de miggle a de street.
Same time me heart go boop
An, Puppa, ah neally dead.
For me tink seh dat him ighniss
Fly up eena po Joe head.

35 An him mussa dah get mad
Meck him stan up eena street
Whe car dah run like fire
An whe four road meet!
But same time Joe raise him han
40 An same time de bus tap bram
An me see one motor car
Dis pass we by so, zam.

Me seh to meself 'Ahoa!
45 Dem haffi wait pon Joe,
An nat one a dem can gwan
So-tell Joe-Joe raise him han,
So-tell fi-me Cousin Joe seh "Move awn!" '

LOUISE BENNETT
Jamaica

Down Beat

A pocket
   myself an arse
a stick of grass
Pinching all to stay alive.
5   Head-lines a sports page
                 Hem-lines a body line
                 Glancing, heckling: all the
                                      time
                 Leaning on Ma Dolly fence
10 Waiting for time to pass
         for the mark to buss
             for the chance
             to ask Chin for trus'.
                         Into Town
15   dark-glasses-glass-cases —
                      staring at faces

staring-listening-moving
Down-Town.
Welcoming Snake Eye
20 Out from jail
with a fete,

   sparing a hasty regret
   for the ting
   he rape
25 While remembering last night wake;
Working on meh sweet mas',
Clanging iron when Carnival in season

   For no reason
   following some demon-
30   stration
Tuning in on the latest rake
or crash programme
Waiting for the next election.
   Talking cricket-talk
35   Jiving on a side walk
   Talking shit-talk
Like say
how many Left-Overs
between tea
40 lunch and tea
   While with a forward defensive
   assertive prod,
   stroking the 'beef' from the valley
Continually moving meh back-side
45 more squarer to the off side
near a gully
   Dividing hours
   into butt-ends, or romy
       hands
50   or marking race

       programmes.
Now an then
as Mighty Suck Eye,
serenading some tourists –
55   hustling some coins
       for a
       four-tirty
Lolling in a snackette
   bush-rum quelling the pain
60   in meh guts
While the Redding
sitting on the dock.

                    Staring at the 'No Hands
                                    Wanted' signs
65   The National Lottery Sold
                                    here signs
                    and the long line –
                    The lime near Marli Street.
      Pulling at meh weed
70   Smoking out meh need
      Cursing dem all
      Forgetting it all

                                    Swaying down the kiss meh
                                                    arse
75   streets
                                    to a rhythm rehearsed in bed
                                    and the down beat in meh
                                                    head
      And over head the sun strumming along,
80   lashing along meh back,
      and I calling dat George
      substituting half measures

      for the w-hole.

                                    VICTOR QUESTEL
                                    Trinidad and Tobago

Me Cyaan Believe It

      Me seh me cyaan believe it
      me seh me cyaan believe it

      Room dem a rent
      me apply widin
5   but as me go een
      cockroach rat an scorpion
      also come een

      Waan good
      nose haffi run
10   but me naw go siddung pon high wall
      like Humpty Dumpty
      me a face me reality

      One little bwoy come blow im horn
      an me look pon im wid scorn
15   an me realize how me five bwoy-picni
      was a victim of de trick
      dem call partisan politricks

an me ban me belly
an me bawl
20 an me ban me belly
an me bawl
Lawd
me cyaan believe it
me seh me cyaan believe it

25 Me daughter bwoy-frien name Sailor
an im pass through de port like a ship
more gran-picni fi feed
an de whole a we in need
what a night what a plight
30 an we cyaan get a bite
me life is a stiff fight
an me cyaan believe it
me seh me cyaan believe it

Sittin on de corner wid me frien
35 talking bout tings an time
me hear one voice seh
'Who dat?'
Me seh 'A who dat?'
'A who a seh who dat
40 when me a seh who dat?'

When yuh teck a stock
dem lick we dung flat
teet start fly
an big man start cry
45 me seh me cyaan believe it
me seh me cyaan believe it

De odder day
me a pass one yard pon de hill
When me teck a stock me hear
50 'Hey, bwoy!'
'Yes, mam?'
'Hey, bwoy!'
'Yes, mam!'
'Yuh clean up de dawg shit?'
55 'Yes, mam.'

An me cyaan believe it
me seh me cyaan believe it

Doris a modder of four
get a wuk as a domestic
60 Boss man move een
an bap si kaisico she pregnant again
bap si kaisico she pregnant again
an me cyaan believe it
me seh me cyaan believe it

65 Deh a yard de odder night
when me hear 'Fire! Fire!'
'Fire, to plate claat!'
Who dead? You dead!
Who dead? Me dead!
70 Who dead? Harry dead!
Who dead? Eleven dead?
Woeeeeeeee
Orange Street fire
deh pon me head
an me cyaan believe it
75 me seh me cyaan believe it

Lawd
me see some blackbud
livin inna one buildin
but no rent no pay
80 so dem cyaan stay
Lawd
de oppress an de dispossess
cyaan get no res

What nex?

85 Teck a trip from Kingston
to Jamaica
Teck twelve from a dozen
an me see me mumma in heaven
Madhouse! Madhouse!

90 Me seh me cyaan believe it
me seh me cyaan believe it

Yuh believe it?
How yuh fi believe it
when yuh laugh
95 an yuh blind yuh eye to it?

But me know yuh believe it
Lawwwwwwwwd
me know yuh believe it

MICHAEL SMITH
Jamaica

Riddym Ravings
(The Mad Woman's Poem)

de fus time dem kar me go a Bellevue
was fi di dactar an de lanlord operate
an tek de radio outa mi head
troo dem seize de bed
5 weh did a gi mi cancer
an mek mi talk to nobady
ah di same night wen dem trow mi out fi no pay de rent
mi haffi sleep outa door wid de Channel One riddym box
an de D J fly up eena mi head
10 mi hear im a play seh

Eh, Eh,
no feel no way
town is a place dat ah really kean stay
dem kudda – ribbit mi han
15 *eh – ribbit mi toe*
mi waan go a country go look mango

fah wen hungry mek King St pavement
bubble an dally in front a mi yeye
an mi foot start wanda falla fly
20 to de garbage pan eena de chinaman backlat
dem nearly chap aff mi han eena de butcha shap
fi de piece a ratten poke
ah de same time de mawga gal in front a mi
drap de laas piece a ripe banana
25 an mi – ben dung – pick i up – an nyam i
a dat time dem grab mi an kar mi back a Bellevue
dis time de dactar an de lanlord operate
an tek de radio plug outa mi head
dem sen mi out, seh mi alright
30 but – as ah ketch back outa street
ah push een back de plug
an ah hear mi D J still a play, seh

Eh, Eh,

no feel no way
35 *town is a place dat ah really kean stay*
dem kudda – ribbit mi han
eh – ribbit mi toe
mi waan go a country go look mango

Ha Haah. . .Haa

40 wen mi fus come a town
mi use to tell everybady 'mawnin'
but as de likkle rosiness gawn outa mi face
nobady nah ansa mi
silence tun rags roun mi bady
45 in de midst a all de dead people dem
a bawl bout de caast of livin
an a ongle one ting tap mi fram go stark raving mad
a wen mi siddung eena Parade
a tear up newspaper fi talk to
50 sometime dem roll up
an tun eena one a Uncle But sweet saaf
yellow heart breadfruit
wid piece of roas saalfish side a i
an if likkle rain jus fall
55 mi get cocanat rundung fi eat i wid
same place side a weh de country bus dem pull out
an sometime mi a try board de bus
an de canductar bwoy a halla out seh
'dutty gal, kum affa de bus'
60 ah troo im no hear de riddym eena mi head
same as de tape weh de bus driva a play, seh

Eh, Eh,
no feel no way
town is a place dat ah really kean stay
65 *dem kudda – ribbit mi han*
Eh – ribbit mi toe
mi waan go a country go look mango
so country bus, ah beg yuh
tek mi home
70 *to de place, where I belang. . .*

an di dutty bway jus ran mi aff
Well dis mawnin, mi start out pon Spanish Town Road,
fah mi deh go walk go home a country
fah my granny use to tell mi how she walk from wes
75 come a town
come sell food
an mi waan ketch home befo dem put de price pon i'

but mi kean go home dutty?
fah mi parents dem did sen mi out clean
80 Ah!
see wan stanpipe deh!
so mi strip aff all de crocus bag dem
an scrub unda mi armpit
fah mi hear di two mawga gal dem laas nite
85 a laugh an seh
who kudda breed smaddy like me?
a troo dem no-know seh a pure nice man
weh drive car an have gun
visit my piazza all dem four o'clock a mawnin
90 no de likkle duty bway dem weh mi see dem a go home
wid
but as mi feel de clear water pon mi bady
no grab dem grab mi
an is back eena Bellevue dem kar mi
95 seh mi mad an a bade naked a street
well dis time de dactar an de lanlord operate
an dem tek de whole radio fram outa mi head
but wen dem tink seh mi unda chloroform
dem put i dung careless
100 an wen dem gawn
mi tek de radio
an mi push i up eena mi belly
fi keep de baby company
fah even if mi nuh mek i
105 me waan my baby know dis yah riddym yah
fram before she bawn
hear de D J a play, seh

Eh, Eh,
no feel no way
110 *town is a place dat ah really kean stay*
dem kudda – ribbit mi han
eh – ribbit mi toe
mi waan go a country go look mango

an same time
115 de dactar an de lanlord
rigger de electric shack
an mi hear de DJ vice bawl out, seh

Murther
Pull up Missa Operator

JEAN 'BINTA' BREEZE
Jamaica

Jus' Like Dat

Yesterday
Ah was mad mad, mad mad,
Mad mad, mad mad mad, mad mad,
Mad mad, mad!
5 Stark ravin' mad!
Yesterday
Ah take off me shirt
An' ah wave it like ah flag,
Jus' like dat!
10 Jus', jus', jus', jus',
Jus' like dat!
Ah wave it like ah flag.
Me good Elite shirt.
Ah wave it like ah flag.
15 Jus' like dat.

Den ah crush it, like ah paper-bag,
Jus' like dat!
Jus, jus', jus', jus',
Jus' like dat!
20 Ah crush it like ah paper-bag!
Den ah throw it,
Jus' like dat!
Yes, jus', jus', jus', jus',
Jus' like dat – ah throw it!
25 Way up in de air, ah throw it,
Jus' like that.
Me good Elite shirt,
Eighteen dollars wort' ah shirt
Flyin' thru' de air,
30 Jus' like dat!

Den ah bawl,
Yes, jus' like dat, ah bawl.

Jus', jus', jus', jus',
Jus' like dat, ah bawl.
35 Like de time ah fall off Webster roof,
An' bust me arse, jus' like dat.
Dat time ah bawl from pain.
Yesterday was different,
Ah jus' bawl, an' bawl, an' bawl again,
40 Jus' like dat!

Den ah wine,
Yes, just' like dat ah wine!
Jus', jus', jus', jus',
Jus' like dat,
45 Ah wine me waist.
Round' an' round', in an' out,
Ah wine down de place,
Jus' like dat!
Den dis woman grab me,
50 Jus' like dat!
Yes, jus', jus', jus', jus',
Jus' like dat – she grab me.
She grab me from behin',
An' she wine,
55 An' I wine,
We wine down de place,
Just' like dat!
Den she disappear,
Just' like dat!
60 Jus', jus', jus', jus',
Jus' like dat – she disappear.
Thru' ah hole in de crowd.

Den ah fella give me ah drink
Jus' like dat!
65 An' ah drink it – jus' like dat!
Yes, jus', jus', jus', jus'
Jus' like dat – ah drink it!
No glass, no chaser, no nothing',
Jus' like dat.
70 An' if yu see de fella,
He smell like ah bag ah shrimp.
But he grinnin',
Yes, he grinnin',
An' I grinnin',
75 Both ah we grinnin',
Jus' like dat!

Den ah jump
Yes, ah jump, jus' like dat!
Jus', jus', jus', jus',
80 Jus' like dat,
Ah jump!
In me boots,

Me good boots,
Me Spanish boots,
85 Reachin' me quite in me ankle,
Ah jump on sixty dollars wort' ah shoe,
Jus' like dat!
An' just' like dat it bus'!
Ah never even know when it bus'!
90 Ah jump!
Like de time ah teaf Shaky plum,
An' he catch me on de tree.
Ah jump down dat time, not up.
Shaky never even know wha' hit him.
95 He roll,
We roll,
Straight in ah ditch.
Like de drain ah fall in yesterday.
Yes, jus' like dat, ah fall in ah drain,
100 An' bus' me face!
Yes, jus' like dat,
Ah nearly dead!

Yesterday
Ah was mad mad, mad mad,
105 Mad mad, mad mad mad, mad mad,
Mad mad, mad!
Stark ravin' mad.
Yesterday was Monday . . .
Yesterday was Tuesday . . .
110 Today is Wednesday . . . Ash Wednesday,
Jus' like dat . . . O' God!

PAUL KEENS-DOUGLAS
Trinidad and Tobago

Brung-skin Gyurl

Week Eighteen
Brung-skin gyurl
I come back
    for good
    ya *knoo* I would
5 ME go back dey?

                 NO WAY

Work slack
Gat the sack
     you knoo I would
10   the chile lookin good
          Is a he?
Help a man unpack nuh

From now, Honey
only warmness and good time for we
15   gyurl
   Baby   No blows
      come see this here mess o' clothes
  AND I bring a suitcase   just for yoo
               Ooo
20 full with records and toothpaste
       Dat food smell good
       (I hope it good)
By the way
      gyurl
25 where yo sister dey
       gyurl

She GORN?!
USA!   I knoo she would
     O GORD I *knoo* she would

Week Twenty-eight
30 Brung-skin gyurl
I gorn again

     when
     I see your sister
     I'll tell her hellooo
35   with a smile
        from yooo

   Got this call

                    from a fren
              in Montrehall
40   say tings bad but I *might* fit
              Now I have me Certifi-kit

      So – miss me a while

                              (care de chile)

      Week Thirty-three
                              GYURL*!*

45   Brung-skin gyurl
              BRUNG-SKIN   GYURL*!!!*

      What yo *say*?   WHO*?*

      is only you-one, she sister, dey?

      (thought *you* was in the USA)

50   listen Sis. . .
                              You and WHO*?*
      where de chile?
                              the *CHILE TOO?!*
                                o.k.. . . You and You
55   best hads miss me a while

      Week Thirty-eight
      Brung-skin gyurl

              BABY O GORD
              NEVER EVER NEVER

60   Had to hop
      couldn't stop

                                              47

from Soufriere to Seattle

TO WHERE EVER EVER

Your feet would drop

Had to find you
Had to find you

GORD IS GOOD
he know I would

So brung-skin gyurl
Am beggin ya
beggin like sin
\ Lemme stay wid ya
lemme lay wid ya
warm and ever present
here in Brooklyn

O GORD GYURL
Everythin
in this wurl gyurl

done gone stone crazy like cattle
Me too
Without you

Yo sister?
good
found a man
behavin like he should

THANK GOD SHE COULD

She and fren
          sen this here battle

o' crazy blackfish-ile
                              Good for you
                                        Honey
                                        Good for me
                              Good for de chile

                              ELSWORTH KEANE
                              St Vincent

Ethiopia under a Jamaican Mango Tree

Jah Brown sit down
unda a mango tree

De anger in a him
jus a swell so.

5 De babylon refuse fi
gi him wuk cause
him is dread locks.

But Jah Brown nah
frown, nat cut no
10 strut, weed cool him
down as him sit-down
unda a Jah mango tree.

Jah Brown pull pan him
weed and think with a
13 gesture 'Me nah wuk fi
nuh babylon.   Babylon will
meet fire.   I man is
son of Jah.   I man is Jah.
I man a guh satter and
20 meditate and plough de land
and I man a guh eat fresh
vegetable, no deadas.   I man
a guh make dis yah mango tree
I temple.   I man a guh hook
25 yah till Jah come fi I.'

So Jah Brown sat
down resting his back
on his mango tree and
his eyes were lost in
30 the ray of smoke.

Ethiopia, Ethiopia, Ethiopia
sounded in his ears
and he arrived at the
Emperor's palace and he
35 was greeted with joy.
A red satin cloak
was placed on his back.
He feasted on fresh
fruits and vegetables.   The
40 Emperor gave him his
granddaughter for his bride.
Jah Brown had returned
and his spirit was filled.

Jah Brown wipe the spittle
45 that had run down his cheek.
'I man is de son of Jah;
I man is Jah; I man is
a Prince among prince; I man
a guh overcome Babylon and
50 babylon
wickedness'.

So Jah Brown nah
frown, weed cool him down,
nah cut no strut, just
55 a sit down unda
Jah mango tree.

OPAL PALMER
Jamaica

Zoo Story – Ja. '76

dis dungle dread say:
'Lion!'
flash de colours
carry thunder on him head;

5 any heart-dead weak-eye
   who try shake him faith
   or break him righteous roots
   him quake dem;
   dis dungle dread roar:
10 'Rastafari!'

   red-green-gold rainbow
   lif' up from Jamdung
   scatter de white thin clouds of heaven –
   rest in I-tyopia. . .
15 but right now, right ya
   earth weird
   creation scared, it turnin' colour. . .
   red-green-gold rainbow
   dis man a-look a swif' way into Zion.

20 spliff use to take him dere
   before –
   but wha'?
   spliff turn a white bone in him hand
   rainbow faith bleach down,
25 city dry him roots to straw.
   him still sight, but no lightning;
   and since all man a-tell lie
   tell him own eye
   confuse him,
30 dis man
   start wear dark glasses
   and checking out de zoo

   lion dem roar like thunder;
   dis dread
35 him head well knot-up
   consider dat dem both from dungle,
   him wonder;
   ' 'dis a de zoo?
   den a which part I-man free?
40 dis cage ya mean captivity –
   fi who?'

   him sight:
   lightning in a lion eye
   flash green-gold-red
45 and dis dread

again now find him rainbow
so
him climb dis last bright hill
down into Zion
50 him answer:
'Rastafari!'
to the charging lion.

KENDEL HIPPOLYTE
St Lucia

A Sit Dung Pon de Wall

a sit dung pon de wall
a watch im a watch mi
is lang lang time a sit dung ya
a watch im a watch mi
5 im pance match im shirt
nat even im shoes look like it tuch dirt
nu shoes pon mi foot
me head well dre'd
rock stone is still mi bed

10 a sit dung pon de wall
a watch im a watch mi

9 to 5
to stay alive
livin in myth
15 eatin shit
im a eat   im a bawl
im a sleep   im a bawl
im a fuu. . . im a bawllll. . .
an dats nat all. . . .
20 a still sit dung pon de wall
is lang lang time a sit dung ya
a watch im a watch mi

sun an rain i naa feel pain
one little wet
25 an im fret to de'th

a sit dung pon de wall a watch im a watch mi
lang lang time

52

a watchin im a watch mi
im check sey mi fool
30 i well well cool

so di manin im pass
a wasnt sittin on de wall
im look north im look south
a could si im 'ave a doubt
35 dis time a was sittin in de street
picking last week food fram out mi teet
im neva andastan
si a neva 'ave nu plan
so im start to run
40 an a car lick im dung

man
is lang lang time a sit dung ya
a watch im a watch mi. . .

MUTABARUKA
Jamaica

Dreadwalk
for the Children

blackman came walking I
heard him sing his
voice was like sand
when the wind dries it

5 said sing for me dreamer
said blackman I cannot
the children are gone
like sand from the quarry

said are you afraid I
10 come closer said blackman
his teeth were like stone
where the pick cuts it

said do you remember
my mouth full of stones he said
15 give I the children
would not step aside

but you holding it wrong I
said love the fist opened
the knife fell away from
20   the raw hand middle

his voice was like wind
when the sea makes it salt
the sun turned a little
the shadows rolled flat
25   blowing closer afraid I
would not step aside

then he held me into
his patience   locked

one

30   now I sing for the children
like wind in the quarry
hear me now
by the wide torn places

I am walking

DENNIS SCOTT
Jamaica

Chain of Days

In the spicing the salting and the blackening
I'm poling up in fires of summerlight.
A tree blooms from my umbilical cord.
I look for a touch from every eye.
5   Darkness the wide shawl with sun's heat,
my mother's songs go from wooden walls.
Humming birds hovering
hibiscus nodding
I dance in the eyes of an open house.

10   On a summer road under swinging palms
      a chain of days showed me bewildered.

Taking the drumming of the sea on land
I take the rooted gestures,
I take the caged growing.

15 Little lamps merely tarnish
   a whole night's darkness.
   Our stories bring out Rolling-Calves
   with eyes of fire and trail of long chain.
   I look for a sign in every face,
20 particularly in my father's face.

   A joy is trapped in me.
   Voices of rainbow birds shower my head.
   I decaptitate my naked toe.
   My eye traps warm dust.
25 I'm born to trot about delivering
   people's words and exchanged favours
   or just grains of corn or sugar or salt.

   Scooped water dances
   in the bucket perched on me.
30 My bellows of breath make leaps of flames.
   I muzzle goat kids in raging sunsets
   and take their mother's milk in morning light.

   Beaten there to remember I know nothing
   I run to school with a page of book
35 and clean toenails and teeth.

   All my homestead eggs go to market.
   Farthings are the wheels that work my world.
   My needs immaterial, I know I'm alien.

   My father stutters before authority.
40 His speeches have no important listener.
   No idea that operates my father
   invites me to approach him.
   And I wash my father's feet in sunset
   in a wooden bowl.

45 And my father's toothless mother is wise.
   My father coaxes half dead cows
   and horses and roots in the ground;
   he whispers to them sweetly and shows
   the fine animal coat he persuaded to shine;
50 he pulls prized yams from soft earth
   like big babies at birth
   to be carried to rich tables.

Confused and lonely I sulk.
Companioned and lost I laugh.
55 I fill hunger with games.

On a summer road under swinging palms
a chain of days showed me bewildered.

I go to the wood
it is a neighbour.
60 I go to the sea
it is a playground.
I circle track marked hills.
I circle feet cut flatlands.

I turn rocks I turn leaves.
65 I hunt stone and nut marbles in woods.
I rob pigeon pairs from high trees.
Wasps inflate my face for a soursop.
I beat big nails into knives.
Tops and wheels and balls come from wood.
70 Yet movement and shape mystify:
I am tantalized.

I understand I'm mistaken
to know I'm truly lovable, and that
my lovable people are truly lovable.
75 I understand something makes me alien.
I wonder why so many seedlings wither
like my father's words before authority.

Wondering, dreaming, overawed, I sit
in the little room with faces like mine.
80 Low lamp light spreads a study
of the past on our faces.
I sleep with the purple of berries
on my tongue, and I warm thin walls.

On a summer road under swinging palms
85   a chain of days showed me bewildered.

I keep back the pig's squeal
or the young ram's holler
when my father takes out their balls
with his own razor.
90 Water I pour washes my father's hands.
I wish my father would speak.

I wish my father would use
magic words I know he knows.
I wish my father would touch me.

95 Past winds have dumped
movements my ancestors made.
I dread my father's days
will boomerang on me.
I want to stop time and go with time.
100 In the hills alone I call to time.
My voice comes back in the trees
and wind. Why isn't there the idea
to offer me as sacrifice like Abraham's son?

My sister goes and washes
105 her breasts in the river.
Like a holy act I wash
in my brothers' dirty water.

On a summer road under swinging palms
a chain of days showed me bewildered.

110 My mother's dead granny brings
medicines to her in dreams.
My mother is a magician.
My mother knows how to ignore my father.
My mother puts food and clothes
115 together out of air. Bush and bark and grasses
work for my mother. She stops
the wickedest vomiting. She tells you
when you haven't got a headache at all.
In the pull of my mother's voice
120 and hands she stings and she washes me.

Put me in bright eye of sunlight
in shadows under broad hats,
on hillside pulling beans,
or chopping or planting,
125 I am restful with my mother.

The smell of sunny fields in my clothes
I meet my mother's newborn in the secret
birth room strong with asafetida.
I say goodbye touching my mother's mother
130 in the yard, her cold face
rigid toward the sky.

Quickfooted in the summer
I come over dust and rocks.
Echo after echo leaves me
135   from the edge of the sea,
from the edge of the sea.

JAMES BERRY
Jamaica

Rolling-Calves: monstrous evil spirits, in the form of
calves, who haunt the countryside at night

Southern Cross
First Movement — Granny Amy

An a must get a chick
But you na get no chick
And a must get a chick
But you na get no chick
5   And a must get a chick
Mi say you nah get no chick!
Pinyaah di hawk is coming down . . .

You know what is
a Leghorn chick?
10   A capon?
A layer?
You know yaws?
You too fool, yaw —
Yaws is a disease
15   that fowls suffer from.
You must be a fowl.

A company of shadow
under the coolie plum tree
each stump a windy tale
20   the dark earth storing history

Here in this place of greening
orange tree, civil orange tree,
coolie plum, naseberry,
the family chickens
25   came to meet their death.
You put the body under

a old pan, leave the head
outside, press down knife to neck
with a clean stroke, let the pan
30   up: see the chicken flatter . . .

And a must get a chick
But you naw get no chick
And a must get a chick
But you naw get no chick
35   And a must get a chick
Mi say you nah get no chick
Pinyaah di hawk is coming down.

Papa kept a nanny goat
in the backyard.
40   I see him milk it still
his fingers deft white milk
answering them in small
clean streams into
the noisy pan.
45   Not a grass was ever
so green as the guinea
grass that goat ate
in that yard. No
mint smell so sharp
50   as the small clump
halfway down the slope
to the back gate.

Is grass and ashes
you take to clean pot
55   you know. You never
know? Beat the clothes
on the big beating stone
beside the pipe, bleach them,
starch them (blue in
60   the starch) and set cleanly
orderly on the line
Not a clothes so white
Not a collar so starch
Not a pot so clean.

65   Papa's carpenter's bench
stood against the orange tree.
Every so often it get shaky
and he shore it up.

What my father could do
70 with a nail and two
sure strokes of a hammer!
I see him plane wood, now,
and the shavings curl
bright browny-red like
75 the sun catch in the wood
and he planing leaves of light,
so and so, so and so,
and the warm steady
noise of the plane, the comfort
80 of making.

   On that bench
one Good Friday I set
a egg white in a jam bottle
to see the shape of the crucified
85 Christ. Not a shape was a shape.
Blue bird, blue bird
in and out the window
blue bird, blue bird
in and out the window
90 Oh Janey I am tired
Take a little girl
and pat her on the shoulder
Take a little girl
and pat her on
95 the shoulder.

Who pat that pat?
My granny had
a big mouth
big nose
100 big bosoms
big belly
big feet.
She restrained
them all.
105 She pat that pat.
It was a waking pat;
a you-haven't-made-
your-bed-yet, pat;
a chile-you-forget-
110 your-drawers-in-the-
bathroom-again, pat;
a never-mind-every-

little-girl-has-
nightmares, pat.
115 I pray God, when
I have grans, I have
a pat like that.

One day down by the beating store
Delores say she wish my mother
120 womb would drop out.
She was a evil-looking woman
head like medusa, plants
shoving clenched fists
from her yellow face
125 like small tough snakes.
Why my mother womb to drop out?
Who not to born?
Which one, as Father Roy
say, would she
130 have savaged in the egg?

At Papa's workbench also
I beat out Pascal's wager,
around ten.
        If God, then hell;
135 if no God, what the hell!
But if hell, well?
If hell, well God.

Papa and Mr Holness built
our house. He looked
140 just like Delores: high cheekbones
yellow bronzing into gold
for he worked
in the sun. He wasn't old
nor young. Just
145 ageless, decent, good, Him
Papa, sieve and saw,
cement and sand and sweat,
These raised the walls
we lived in, set
150 a roof firmly astride,
When man and man
build so, it give a
meaning to abide.

PAMELA MORDECAI
Jamaica

61

Fly

ef a ketch im
a mash im
ef a ketch im
a mash im
5 *ef a ketch im . . . .*

Will you walk into my parlour
Said the spider to the fly
It's the prettiest snugliest parlour
That ever you did spy . . .
10 And I
the fly
inspecting your web
this skein now then that
put my
15 microscope eye
through its intricate weave
saw valleys of cloud
blue and serene
saw acres of grass
20 sheltered and green.
Ephemeral and light
I rested my life
and dazzled
I watched
25 you wove me inside
and dazzled
I slept
my crysalis sleep . . . . .

I woke up inside
30 no more dazzled and green.
Awake and alert
unfolding my wings
I stretched . . . . . .
But your skeins
35 not delicate now
resistant and strong
they wove me inside
I am trapped
I can't move
40 I can't butterfly
fly . . . .

And you
perched outside
your eyes large and clear
45 you see acres of green
you see valleys of cloud
you can move
you can fly . . . .
Now I look
50 through the web
I look into the void
I see numberless flies
training microscope eyes
through intricate weave
55 ANANSI I cry
ANANSI – SI – SI I hear
the sky is too vast
how it scatters my cry
the sky is too clear
60 it hides my despair
they can't hear
they can't see
with their microscope eye . . . .

ef a ketch im
65 *a mash im*
ef a ketch im
a mash im

A ketch im.   im. . .im

VELMA POLLARD
Jamaica

Sister Mary and the Devil

I was going down the road
and the two o'clock sun
only beating down on the
roses on Brother Williams wreath
5 till them curl up like them want to
sleep,
and is only me and God
alone
Going down the road.

10   the dust was powdering
mi clean white shoes
when I look down
and see me shadow double.
I know him was the devil.
15   him never have to tell me
because mi blood start to run
and stop
and heavy down mi step
and the ground leave
20   mi foot
and mi heart like it want
stop
and I wash wid cold sweat.

The devil himself
25   a tall man in full black
with a hat that cover him
face like a umbrella
then him take Brother Williams
wreath from me
30   and him hold mi round mi waist
and fire catch in mi body
and I shame and hide mi face
and then him talk for the first
time
35   and it was there
Sister Mary died
when the devil
in him
satan voice
40   hold on to
the wreath and said
today is mine Sister Mary
let the dead
Bury the dead.

LORNA GOODISON
Jamaica

Klickity–Klack

When last you see the city street
looking so sweet?
It really hard on them aching feet
but when last you see the city streets
5   looking so sweet?
Young thing; old thing; Old time something in a come again shot
parch nuts, cigarettes – ital pot
Georgetown pavements looking real hot.
10 Klickity Klack, Klickity Klack along long line
by the ice cream shop
another long line by the gasolene spot-
Klickity Klack, Klickity Klack.
Since the gasolene shortage lots of
15 stretch jeans in town
shoe–makers, sweet sellers are all
around.
Klickity Klack, Klickity Klack
shoe-heel and pavement all two knock.
20 Klickity Klack, Klickity Klack
thousands typefaces on a letter press block
tapping out history, living out the facts
Klickity Klack, Klickity Klack
get in on the news, get in on the facts
25 Klickity Klack, Klickity Klack.

12.30 and the cinemas all sold out
with the blackout at home
where hungry faces sit glum
it is better in the 12.30 to come
30 where chinee and yankee make you live out their life
story
buy parch nut, buy cigarette,
'two balls and a pun'
spend the five dollars or twenty but
35 hurry
blackmarket your ticket: four dollars
for house
seven dollars balcony
three hours from reality in New York or Chinee
40 Klickity Klack, Klickity Klack
letter-press faces type out the facts
Klickity Klack, Klickity Klack
shoe-heel and pavement all two knock.

Not everybody walking, up and down
45 the city. Some cool out on the pavement
with a tray and 'nough stocks
foreign biscuits, foreign toffees
foreign chocolates and bubble gum packs
accumulating money
50 the whole city is on attack
grandmothers, grandchildren
old and young it's a fact
Klickity Klack, Klickity Klack
shoe heel and pavement all two knock
55 and the sound that they make like
a letter-press block
printing out history as they live through
the acts

A old time police-man, he done murder a
60 youth,
now awaiting investigation
runs a footwear booth
He sits on the pavement with lots
of foreign shoes
65 barefoot children passing, digging
no blues
young sweeties walk by in ones and twos

Young girls take over the whole Georgetown scene,
the gov't uniform is lemon and green
70 in every sidewalk crowd they bright up the scene
with nice firm legs
holding promise between
and an innocent look like a virgin queen.
Klickity Klack, Klickity Klack
75 Water St, Regent St, the Aracde or Bourda
Green
thousands of touching bodies whispers
fulfilling dreams
a taxi-driver eye-up a woman right
80 pon she pants seam
he han full of twenties if you
know what I mean

'Panties' 'Brassieres' 'Corn-Curls' they shout
buyers and sellers moving about
85 outside public beer pubs
lots of Guiness stout, twenty dollars a

bottle that you lift to your mouth
then sit on your motor-scooter
ride your fancy clothes about.
90 Not everybody got money, some got
to tout. At the taxi stand
not a taxi going South.
Everybody get vex and start run up they
mouth.

95 Parchnut in glass cases with electric light
Gary on Cambell Ave selling
cigarettes day and night
everybody hustling a dollar cause
things well tight,
100 the school ent have school girls
once they body get ripe.

Klickity Klack, Klickity Klack
Money, Money, Money,
hustling is fact
105 Klickity Klack, Klickity Klack
Sex and money
and be happy you're black
even coolie people them
caught in the attack
110 they selling out culture to full
a money sack
A pandit get caught in a cocaine trap
Klickity Klack, Klickity Klack
Georgetown 1987 under cultural attack.

115 Klickity Klack

RAS MICHAEL JEUNE
Guyana

Elegy, Lament

Black Friday 1962

were some who ran one way.
were some who ran another way.
were some who did not run at all.
were some who will not run again.
5 And I was with them all,
when the sun and streets exploded,
and a city of clerks
turned a city of men!
Was a day that had to come,
10 ever since the whole of a morning sky,
glowed red like glory,
over the tops of houses.

I would never have believed it.
I would have made a telling repudiation.
15 But I saw it myself
and hair was a mass of fire!
So now obsessed I celebrate in words
all origins of creation, whores and virgins:
I do it with a hand upon a groin
20 swearing this way, since other ways are false!

For is only one way, one path, one road.
And nothing downward bends, but upward goes,
like leaves to sunlight, trees to the sun itself.
All, all who are human fail,
25 like bullets aimed at life,
or the dead who shoot and think themselves alive!

Behind a wall of stone beside this city,
mud is blue-grey when ocean waves are gone,
in the midday sun!
30 And I have seen some creatures rise from holes
and claw a triumph like a citizen,
and reign until the tide!

Atop the iron roof tops of this city
I see the vultures practising to wait.

35 And everytime, and anytime,
   in sleep or sudden wake, nightmare, dream,
   always for me the same vision of cemeteries, slow funerals,
   broken tombs, and death designing all.

   True, was with them all,
40 and told them more than once:
   in despair there is hope, but there is none in death.
   Now I repeat it here, feeling a waste of life,
   in a market-place of doom, watching the human face!

MARTIN CARTER
Guyana

Shaker Funeral

   Sorrow sin-
   bound, pelting din
   big chorusclash
   o' the mourners,
5 eyes red
   with a shout for the dead,
   yelling crash-
   ing sadness in
   the dusty tread
10 o' the mourners.

   Sweet Mother gone
   to the by and by,
   follow her to the brink o' Zion.

   Wave wave
15 as they roared to grave
   a drench song –
   soulthunder –
   was *aymens* through
   the wind, shrieks flew,
20 and eyes were strong;
   for 'twas madness gave
   them dirge, that grew
   made thunder.

   Drums, flags,
25 pious rags o'
   robes stenching
   sweat;

mitre o'tattered
straw, bamboo crozier
30 wagged by wind's clenching–
deathwind that bragged
sorrow, smattered
o' sweat.

Saints in blue
35 bathrobes flew
about the ranks
o' the sinners,
and froth-lipped virgins
with powdered skins
40 and frocks that stank
with the slime and the stew
from the purged away sins
o' the sinners;

And heads were white
45 in starched cloth. . .Bright
was the blood from the eyes
o' the candles;
and the 'horn of the Ram
of the great I Am'
50 spoke hoarse in cries. . .
and crowned with the light
o' the Judah Lamb
were the candles.

Lord delivered Daniel
from shame's mouth,
(o strong, o strong roll Jordan).
Lord deliver our Mother
gone to the Glory Home,
gone to the Glory Home, gone to Zion.

60 All God's brothers
were loud, and the ten
holy lampers were
reeking in smoke;
and the 'valley of sod-
65 and-shadow,' Staff-Rod,
was blenched as the canker-
ing sweat o' men
and the reeking o' God
in the smoke.

70   His willing be,
       Mother gone,
       Jordan deep,
       but her soul is strong.
       Follow her to the brink o' Zion.

75 And now the grave
      was washed in a wave
      o' wails and a
      city o' stars

      that dribbled and burned
80 in the tears that turned
      hot sins, on the smoke-white pillars. . .
      But their sorrow was yells,
      and their faith was brave
      as the blood-blemished lambs
85 piled big on the grave
      their city o' wax and stars.

      Sweet Mother gone,
      King o' Mansions-over-Jordan.
      O strong. . .
90 Leave her safe on the brink o' Zion.

ELSWORTH KEANE
St Vincent

Trees His Testament
A goodbye for Daley

      Daley's dead; dust now, gone for good
      Far over Jordan side
      Left his body this side
      Of the cold river.
5 Dead now, gone for good
      Nobody see him till Kingdom come
      And the trumpet call beyond the river
      And the roll call.
      Gone for good,
10 Lips greedy once for a woman's breast
      Still now and silent
      Pasture for the worm
      Then dust.

Daley was a plumber,
15 Served his time to Hard Up,
Hungry Belly walked beside him
Never left him quiet
Through the slum he had for home
From door to door he asked
20 If they wanted toilets fixed
And they laughed for the toilet wasn't theirs anyway.
Walked and tramped from door to door
Raising cash for peace of mind,
Pocket full is belly full
25 Belly full is peace of mind.
Hungry Belly never left him.
Grinned and gnawed and never left him
Who would mend what wasn't his anyway?
Plumber's dead now, gone for good.
30 Daley's dead.

Hungry Belly restless talked
When he saw his Daley buy
Paint and canvas for a picture
For a picture when a plumber had to live.
35 But the painter was a-seeking
For the something that he couldn't tell about
That he knew inside himself he must search and search and find,
Knock and knock until he find
Past the questions and divisions
40 Past the doubtings and the troubles
Past the doors and rows of doors
Till at last he saw it all in the trees;
They were quiet and at peace in the pastures
And beside the waters still
45 And upon the mountain side
Where the drought would parch the roots
And the hurricane would walk in the Summer,
Trunks and roots were hard and torn
Branches broken short, and twisted,
50 Just to keep a footing there
Just to be a living tree.
Plumber's hand and painter's eye,
Plumber's dead and gone for good,
Daley's dead.

55 Over now the search for silver
   Gone away is Hungry Belly
   Off to find a fresh companion;
   Dust the feet that walked beside him,
   Turned to dust the plumber's hands
60 But the trees still stand together
   Like they're shouting over Jordan,
   And, look see—how cedar trees
   Do shade a garden in that place.
   And upon that skull-shaped hill top
65 When the eye of day is clean
   Stand two trees with bitter bearing
   And between the two a tree
   One between the two that lifts
   Bright flowering.

PHILIP SHERLOCK
Jamaica

On his Grandmother's Death, news of which he received in Lans-en-Vercours

Amidst this blue of skies and white of snows
   I read the note from occidental hills
   From where the slug-trailed custard-apple grows
And the bastard bombay mango daily fills
5   Its olive skin with juices that attain
   The cycle's point of closure where fullness kills,
From where her trees so blindly know the gain
   That sunlight brings, that soil provides, I hear
   That she is dead.

10   Vibration of tolling bell again
I feel, first felt with her at funeral
   Of Bishop O'Hare, the sapling I beneath her shade
   Not dreaming yet that time that made me tall
Would bend her to the earth and with its spade

15   Plough her ashes back to bless the soil
   While her spirit's crystal fountain played
Above the roughcast ocean, above the toil
   Of lovers young who stride on grass that covers
   The bones and melted breasts where coil
20 Fingers and worms of their dead brothers.

The dead sea fountain sings to me with still
Persisting shape, Valery's perpetual motion hovers
In his voiced words shaping the silence on a hill
Above the central sea;
25   but you whose death
Disturbs these snows, scorching cold eyes that fill
The soul with wonder and with salt, even without breath
You live, not an impressed scent among yellow pages,
Not conjured back by any reader's breath,

30 But fountain of your being plays against the rages
Of time's raucous sea, the rose you were and are
And ever will be is your self still bursting through the ages.

JOHN FIGUEROA
Jamaica

Hard Drought

We marched in Butler's
barefoot made battalions
in a damned time
on the slave world's slipping edge;
5 our arms were rhetoric
and they shot us down
and scattered us to the trade winds;
we shook the pillars of the place and wept.

Williams called us
10 and we thought we'd won;
we set him on the golden stool,
gave him Kingdom upon Kingdom
of the heart; our pride and love
ringed him with janizaries.

15 Confusion fell upon us
as we learned on the years' marches
that he was not ours but history's ruin,
his homing instinct's back to barracoons
and slave plantations.
20 Damballa laughed
Jehovah sneered
They sent no Moses season
no one of Toussaint's valour
nor Joshua's genius for the craft of war.

25 We were a mob;
   our barricades fell down on our own braying
   Jackals have whinnied in the lion's lair.
   A cruel cunning lodged that grappe
   of fools where Butler lodged
30 a generation gone; their rank piss
   fouled the old man's tattered sheets.

   This veteran of griefs, betrayals, shames
   snarls in the ancestral void
   where the Middle passage flung us
35 on our knees. And in one whole ear
   I hear the moles purr in the silent dark
   among the stones . . . . these wretched murmurations . . . . . .

   Don't mock me about dreams
   I am too old.
40 Don't sneer of prophecies
   count me among the numberless dead
   this grisly century.
   I've eaten so much history that I belch
   boloms of years to come.
45 Drunk each day's carnival
   I leer and squint at time telescoped
   in Jesus' spear-cleft side.
   We shall not build
   a kingdom of this world that is not ours

50 Station by station throughout history
   the ground is bloody; the hero's face
   stamped on the woman's napkin masked in blood.

ERIC ROACH
Trinidad and Tobago

Verse in August
For Frank Collymore

   knock drum
   draw bow
   on fiddle strings
   let rhythm jump
5   and catgut screech
   let all time jig
   a kalinda and reel

these august freedom days
let dead bones rise
10 and dance their own bongos

who'll dance my death farewell?
who'll trample me a rhythm on my grave?
    'bongo macedonia
    viniway viniway bongo'
15 not my tall sons
they have not seen nor heard
that macabre rime of death
and if they did
   i could not answer their disdain
20 they have inherited another season
  in this uprooted suburb
  of folk from villages and slums
where dusks brood secret hatreds
  and faces are tight shut
25 from love and friendship.

my life began among kind folk
  whose barefoot indigence was whole
  as rocks and springs, whose love
  nourished life's roots
30   whose labour was
a cutlass hoe and spade
in plots of corn and yams.
i knew some legendary men
  i know them still
35 they're fast in file on film
  a thought reanimates them
whom only my death will bury
for they're mine, they're mine
until my body lays me down.

40 i knew that cruel cunning man
  old pa ben gordon grumbling in his beard
  mumbling evil at the world
threatening jumbie obeah
  and harder vengeances
45 on those humbugging him
  the world humbugged him.
thumping his stick on ground
railing at me always railing
  pouring all molten hell into my bones
50   at first i feared and then i hated him.

my mother said the devil fathered him
   she was his kin
   as real as life
these 50 years he's mummied in me
55 his stick his greybeard
and his guile and grumbling.

i saw br'angas once
   kneel under killing blows
his poui warding death.
60   *'mumma, mumma.*
       you son in de grave arready
       he down in de grave arready'
he rose from that
his fierce eyes bleeding vengeance
65 his squat thick body leaping
   the stick flailing,
the drums choked on a note
and his foes fled.

rum drums and singing men
65   gambash in the gayelle
   carray!. ah bois garcon!
   ah ah! ah ah!
     'hooray horrah cutoutah
     how much hero you kill in arima?'
70 bloodshed on freedom day
rum drums and broken heads.
ah august kalindas!
all that long ended
but i have it still
75   a bright splash on the mind.

i knew men pushing out to sea
at dusk in bare canoes
wave skimming wooden shells
i watched the steady rhythm of their oars
80 diminishing on the sea scape
till darkness took them
a-morning they returned
naked as fish,
wet as the dripping sea
85 summoning us with conches
and slow haul up of boats out of the tide.

hot days in glittering bays
white-waved fawn-sanded and
   green-fringed with palm and sea grape trees
90 the girls loved under the sea grape trees
   all that pure loving for the loving's sake
   the animal ecstasy of the ignorant blood.
the days stand up to bless me
   as i die
95 bedded on my dying century
dreaming the century's youth
   in a good place that's gone
   among the folk i loved
while my own death
100 howls from a mangy dog
haunting these barren streets.

what's all my witness for?
why do i wear the poor folk and the years?
eh brother what's the score?
105 is the game won or lost?
will i know now
at the breaking bitter last?
do old men know?

ERIC ROACH
Trinidad and Tobago

For Harry Simmons

Brown, balding, with a lacertilian
jut to his underlip,
with spectacles thick as a glass paperweight
and squat, blunt fingers,
5 waspish, austere, swift with asperities,
with a dimpled pot for a belly from the red clay of Piaille.
Eyes like the glint of sea-smoothed bottled glass,
his knee-high khaki stockings,
brown shoes lacquered even in desolation.

10 People entered his understanding
like a wayside country church,
they had built him themselves.
It was they who had smoothed the wall
of his clay-coloured forehead,

15 who made of his rotundity an earthy
useful object
holding the clear water of their simple troubles,
he who returned their tribal names
to the adze, mattock, midden and cookingpot.

20 A tang of white rum on the tongue of the mandolin,
a young bay, parting its mouth,
a heron silently named or a night-moth,
or the names of villages plaited into one map,
in the evocation of scrubbed back-yard smoke,
25 and he is a man no more
but the fervour and intelligence
of a whole country.

Leonce, Placide, Alcindor,
Dominic, from whose plane vowels were shorn
30 odorous as forest,
ask the charcoal-burner to look up
with his singed eyes,
ask the lip-cracked fisherman three miles at sea
with nothing between him and Dahomey's coast
35 to dip rain-water over his parched boards
for Monsieur Simmons, *pour* Msieu Harry Simmons,
let the husker on his pyramid of coconuts
rest on his tree.

Blow out the eyes in the unfinished portraits.

40 And the old woman who danced
with a spine like the 'glory cedar',
so lissome that her veins bulged evenly
upon the tightened drumskin of the earth,
her feet nimbler than the drummer's fingers,
45 let her sit in her corner and become evening
for a man the colour of her earth,
for a cracked claypot full of idle brushes,
and the tubes curl and harden,
except the red,
50 except the virulent red!

His island forest, open and enclose him
like a rare butterfly between its leaves.

DEREK WALCOTT
St Lucia

79

Stone for Mikey Smith
(Stoned to death on Stony Hill, 1954–1983)

When the stone fall that morning out of the johncrow sky
it was not dark at first . that opening on to the red sea humming
but something in my mouth like feathers . blue like bubbles
carrying signals & planets & the sliding curve of the world like a water picture in a raindrop when the pressure . drop

5   When the stone fall that morning out of the johncrow sky
i couldn't cry out because my mouth was full of beast & plunder
as if i was gnashing badwords among tombstones
as if that road up stony hill . round the bend by the church

yard . on the way to the post office . was a bad bad dream
10 & the dream was like a snarl of broken copper wire zig zagg.
ing its electric flashes up the hill & splitt. ing spark & flow.
ers high. er up the hill . past the white houses & the ogogs bark.
ing all teeth & fur. nace & my mother like she up. like she up. like she up

side down up a tree like she was scream. like she was scream. ing no & no
15 body i could hear could hear a word i say . ing . even though
there were so many poems left & the tape was switched on & runn. ing &
runn. ing & the green light was red & they was standin up there & ever.
                    where
in london & amersterdam & at unesco in paris & in west berlin & clapp.
                    ing &

clapp. ing & clapp. ing & not a soul on stony hill to even say amen
20 & yet it was happening happening happening . the fences begin
to crack in i skull . & there was loud bodoooooooooooooooooooogs like
guns goin off . them ole time magnums . or like a fireworks a dreadlocks
was on fire . & the gaps where the river comin down & the drei gully

where my teeth use to be smilin . & i tuff gong tongue
25 that use to press against them & parade pronunciation . now un-
announce
& like a black wick in i head & dead . &
it was like a heavy heavy riddim low down in i belly . bleedin dub . &
there was like this heavy heavy black dog thump. in in i chest & pump.
                    ing

murdererrrrrrrrrrrrrrrrrrrrrrrrrrrrrrrrrrrrrrrrrrrrrrrrrrrrrrrrrrrrrrrrrrrrrrr

30 & i throat like dem tie. like dem tie. like dem tie a tight tie around
it . twist. ing my name quick crick . quick crick . & a never wear neck

80

tie yet . & a hear when de big boot kick down i door . stump
in it foot pun a knot in de floor. board . a window slam shut at de back
a mi heart . de itch & ooze & damp a de yard in my silver tam.

35 bourines closer & closer . st joseph marching bands crash. ing &
closer &

bom si. cai si. cai si. ca boom ship bell . bom si. ca boom ship bell

& a laughin more blood &
spittin out

40 lawwwwwwwwwwwwwwwwwwwwwwwwwwwwwwwwwwwwwwwwd

& i two eye lock to the sun & the two sun starin back black from de grass
& i bline to de butterfly fly

in

45 & it was like a wave on stony hill caught in a crust of sun
light

& it was like a matchstick schooner into harbour
muffled in the silence of it wound

50 .
& it was like the blue of speace was filling up the heavens with it thunder
& it was like the wind was grow. ing skin

.

the skin had hard hairs . hardering

55 .
it was like marcus garvey rising from his coin . stepping towards his
people
crying dark

& every mighty trod he word. the ground fall dark & hole be.
hine him like it was a bloom ex. ploding sound . my ears was bleed.

60 ing sound

.

& i was quiet now because i had become that sound
the sun. light morning washed the coral limestone harsh

against the soft volcanic ash. i was

81

65 & it was slipping past me into water & it was slipping past me into
root. i was

& it was
slipping past me into flower & it was
ripping upwards into shoot. i was

70 & every politrician tongue in town was lash
ing me with spit & cut. rass wit & ivy whip & wrinkle jumbimum
it was like warthog . grunt. ing in the ground

& children running down the hill run right on through the splash
of pouis that my breathe. ing made when it was howl & red & bubble
75 & sparrow twits pluck tic & tap. worm from the grass

as if i man did have no face . as if i man did never in this place

.
When the stone fall that morning out of the johncrow sky
i could not hold it brack or black it back or block it off or limp
80 away or roll it from me into memory or light or rock it steady into night
be

cause it builds me now with leaf & spiderweb & soft and crunch & like
the
powderwhite & slip & grit inside your leather. boot & fills my blood
with deaf my bone with hobble. dumb & echo. less neglect neglect
neglect neglect

&
85 lawwwwwwwwwwwwwwwwwwwwwwwwwwwwwwwwwwwwwwwwwwwwd

i am the stone that kills me

EDWARD KAMAU BRATHWAITE
Barbados

Reggae for Radni
To the memory of Walter Rodney

yu noh si ow di cloud
dem just come satta pan mi dream
sit upon mi dream
like a daak silk-screen
5 a daak silk-screen
ovah di vizshan I ad seen
di vizshan I ad seen
di vizshan I ad seen . . . .

Some may say dat Waltah Radni
10   woz a victim of hate
some wi seh dat im gaan
through heaven's gate
some wi seh dat Waltah Radni
shouldn' tek-up histri weight
15   and goh carry it pan im back
like im did wear im anarack

but look ow di cloud
dem just come satta pan mi dream
sit upon mi dream
20   like a shout ar a scream
a shout ar a scream
ar a really ugly scene
dat awake mi fram di dream
an alert mi to di scheme . . .

25   some may say dat Waltah Radni
woz a prizinah of fate
some wi seh dat im gaan
through di heroes gate
some wi seh sat Waltah Radni
30   couldn't tek histri wait
soh im tek it aaf im back
an goh put it pan im lap
an goh fall in a trap
an soh Burnham get e drap

35   you noh si ow mi dream
come just get blown to smidahreen
blown to smidahreen
inna di miggle a di dream
di miggle a di dream
40   before di people dem come een
di people dem come een
di people dem come een. . .

Some may say dat Waltah Radni
woz noh shaak fi di sea
45   an all dat im did want
woz fi set im people free
wid di werkaz an di pezants
im shoulda kawpahrate
but like a fish to di ook
50   im goh bite pan Burnham bait

LINTON KWESI JOHNSON
Jamaica

Maurice

In Memory of Maurice Bishop

There was never any doubt about the incline you chose,
brambly with hope as the island-home you went back to,
but blocked in by house-treachery and a raised arm of eaglets.

In spite of the clang of the claws from the eyrie in the north,
5 murder by mongoose, and later, the blasted bodies under the
                                        bleachers,
the new jewel seemed firmly set in place to do all the good it could.

There's a happiness that the truth brings, and sometimes, a dead
                                              loss;
10 both startle our islands, but if both aren't spliced and read wisely,
stagnation flourishes. You cleared the way for the chance of a
                                             choice

which was wrenched from us by lies, lawlessness and quick metal;
not what you meant by the truthful gift you gave us,
15 *not* what the wisdom of the dialectic intended. But dreadful loss,
                                           only.

And mangling capture. Things are broken up and elliptical, now.
Next to nothing is left of your stitching and cross-stitching and
                                           annealing,
20 while much rides roulette on nutmegs, tourist sand and bootprints.

ANDREW SALKEY
Jamaica

For Indira Gandhi

You let the hawk in you
break loose.
That, you seemed to think,
would bring the dove back
5 to a disastrous sky.
Perhaps you stood too firm
and so were unbalanced
when you tried to throw
a lariat over a lion's head.

10   You wanted the garden whole.
What you saw as weeds
might only have been flowers
of a different kind;
and the wild horses
15   that would not be stabled
nor join the herd
were perhaps lions
that would have given too many tears.

For some, Indira,
20   You still are,
a bright mark in the sky, your memory
a suddenly appearing star
in their heart's gloom.
For others, you were
25   the sky's starring sore,
the sore only
hate's keen surgery
could have removed.

Raincloud in drought,
30   or monsoon,
sore or star,
you made your mark high,
upon the heavens.
You were spectacular,
35   and when you fell, all
looked your way
again, and wondered.

MICHAEL AARONS
Guyana

Carousel
For Namba Roy, 1910–1961

I often spin around with you and hear
the fragile music of a carousel;
I feel your black arms round me in a heavy sweep
of closeness, taking me up on notes which fall
5   like eggs through water.

I am older now
and you have fallen from the garish horse
a long time since, and I am holding on
with thin brown fingers. Do you know
10 it's been a quarter century since you
(with your voice like the man who plays God in the movies)
kissed me? I don't remember your kisses.
I remember you wearing striped pyjamas
and waving to me from the ward – your great hand
15 scooping a half-circle out of nothing;
how my brother almost choked on a *Lifesaver*
until a male nurse turned him upside down
and out come the white mint with the hole
that saved him.

20   I dreamed you died, and when I woke
my mother was by the bed. "How will I light
the fire?" she said. I didn't know.

It was cold in our house; our breath came out
round as balloons and dissolved till we breathed
25 again. We learned to accommodate spaces
as you must have learned to accommodate. . .
but no. Where there is no place to put things,
no place for your bones or your slippers or my words
there cannot be a place for spaces.
30 It must be fine to know only lack of substance –
the round emptiness in an angel's trumpet –
and still hear music.

               I have the things you made
and she has made us see you in them.
35 I have the ivory statues and the pictures
telling stories of African ancestors,
a birth, flights into Egypt. In your work
I find the stillness of your eyes and mouth,
the stillness which is always at the centre
40 of the spinning ball we hurl high and long.

I often spin around with you and hear
the fragile music of a carousel.
My horse would gallop forward if I let him
but I prefer the swinging back to where

45 we were, slow undulations round and back
    to identical place. I prefer to see
    your black hands with mine on a crimson mane
    which will never be swept back by the wind.

LUCINDA ROY
Jamaica

Hey, Alfie

    hey, Alfie
    as the cracked blue piano notes
    tinny off into cacophany
    of microphoned harshness
5   through a beard,
    as the trumpet
    highpeaks Ujaama
    to Uhuru

    the cracked notes
10 and split banknotes
    among spilt coffee
    and cracked plates
    counterpoint
    cracking balls
15 as crushed balls wail a song
    for manhood

    hey, Alfie
    and we try to sing
    a song of joy
20 in the joyless air
    of smokefilled
    trashfilled coinclinking
    proletarian euphoria
    blowing our minds
25 with the invective notes
    of the horn
    forcing a logic
    like the fullextended
    slide of a chatanooga
30 trombone
    singing a song of blues
    against brother

87

with no melodic pattern
but an echo
35 of explosions
on a slackskinned drum
drum
drummed by a slack-
wristed drummer

hey, Alfie
as the mind musicians
compose in their
concerthall void
in their middlesearch
45 emptiness of pool
in their cadence
of subliminal pain
as limpwristed drummers
miss their beats
50 while looking beat
smiling beatific
behind glazed eyes
of the committed
behind dark shades
55 which screen
past and heritage
and boldly blow bluesy
Imami, the Id
the dejected,
60 the rejected

hey,   e
        Al
            fi-

ANSON GONZALEZ
Trinidad and Tobago

Screws Loose

I do not wish to sit and smile
too sweetly where the pavement ends
nor set small windy fires at Papine
nor scrupulously cleanse myself in streams
5 guttering too slowly
gathering stench on stench

I do not wish to mumble as I go
gesturing wildly as the voice grows loud
eyes staring wide
10 and crude uneasy laugh

mad people whisper late
sane peoples early dreams
beware my inmost thoughts
that wait mad mind's release

15 too much too soon
the mind rejects it all
uncensored now and overflowing here
flotsam and jetsam mixed with precious pearl

and so my love my seraph dear go home
20 mad women whisper sane men's names
and not in jest
   leave me my dreams of growing calmly old
turning thin ages in moth ridden books
rocking my evening bones
25 watching each sun go down

VELMA POLLARD
Jamaica

Friends

Ah boy
Ah boy
To know yuhself
Know yuh friends
5 Yes boy
Ah boy
When yuh loss
Can' replace
Ah boy
10 When yuh muddah
Dead. . .
Ah boy
Uhuh
Uhuh
15 Who come
To de house

Bow 'e head
In grief
Shake yuh han'
20 Sympat'ize
Fuh yuh feel
Stan' up quiet
Round' de coffin
Offer a prayer
25 From 'e heart
Fuh she soul
Ah boy
Ah boy
Follow she
30 Pon foot
In buggy
In car
To de church
Ah boy
35 Ah boy
Sing de hymns
Chant de psalms
Pray
Ah, Ah boy
40 Walk behin' yuh
To de grave
In de sun
In de rain
Watch yuh strain
45 To lif' de ol' lady
Let she down
Ah boy
Ah boy
Hear de hoe
50 Hit de rock
Clock, clock
Again an' again
Ah boy
Clock
55 Drag
Clack
Scrape. . .
Clock
Ah boy. . .
60 De soun'
De las' soun'
Ah. . .

<pre>
        Put. . .
        De wreaths. . .
        Put
        'E han
     70 Pun yuh shoulder
        Walk away
        Ah boy
        Meet yuh home
        Squeeze yuh han'
     75 Tek a drink
        Ah boy
        Wish yuh strength
        Courage
        Ah boy
     80 Yes boy
        Dem is frien'
        True frien'
        Ah boy
        Ah boy
     85 Uhuh!
        Uhuh!
</pre>

BRUCE ST JOHN
Barbados

Memorial Blues for Billie Holiday

<pre>
   One must burn to sing
   peeling layers of heart to the blue note
           leaf layer from leaf
   the pearl must strip
 5   pure blue note.

   The sick acrid-acid blues
   bitter after-taste of hurt feelings
           bruised raw
           awakes to a high
10   dry note.

           Singing,
               swinging songs
           with hate for words
   shattering the clatter of coffee house chatter
15   the shrill blue notes
</pre>

         ignite to star
and the shrieking soul is pared
         note by note
         to the pallid chrysalid heart-thing.

20   Are we even now aware
         that with each new note
another petal of the heart-rose loosened?

         Who will understand why
         even the red rose
25   under your hand turned to blue?

                              ALEC BEST
                              Guyana

For the D

'To John Coltrane, the heaviest spirit'
Black Music, Leroi Jones/Imamu Baraka

                    Don
         may I learn the shape of that hurt
         which captured you nightly into
         dread city, discovering through
5   streets steep with the sufferer's beat;

         Teach me to walk through jukeboxes
         & shadow that broken music
         whose irradiant stop is light;
         guide through those mournfullest journeys

10   I back into harbour Spirit
         in heavens remember we now
         & show we a way in to praise,
         all seekers to-gether, one-heart:

         and let we lock conscious when wrong
15   & Babylon rock back again:
         in the evil season sustain
         o heaviest spirit of sound.

                              ANTHONY McNEILL
                              Jamaica

Valley Prince
for Don D

Me one, way out in the crowd,
I blow the sounds, the pain,
but not a soul
would come inside my world
5   or tell me how it true.
I love a melancholy baby,
sweet, with fire in her belly;
and like a spite
the woman turn a whore.
10 Cool and smooth around the beat
she wake the note inside me
and I blow me mind.

Inside here, me one
in the crowd again,
15 and plenty people
want me blow it straight.
But straight is not the way; my world
don' go so; that is lie.
Oonu gimme back me trombone, man:
20 is time to blow me mind.

MERVYN MORRIS
Jamaica

South Trumpeter

Today, again, he is there –
no wild paranoid gaze to betray,
no palm turned upward
for pennies,
5   no sad haze of defeat;
his is only a prideful stare
in the face of things, aware
that a foolish time wilts and dies
beneath its own ways.

10 When ready, he
stands, and with trumpet levelled
at the crossroads of time, this
man-god blows his mind's fire.
Down it comes, engulfing

15 cities that crack and crumble, souls
    writhe, are raised, are freed;
    down it comes with each burst
    and the whole earth quakes,
    and prisons are broken
20 by those staccato blasts.

    But he alone knows
    that these piercing notes
    may be daggers too,
    to touch a heart that's hard
25 or rend that sky of blue.

LEROY CALLISTE
Trinidad and Tobago

Canto I

    ashes head to toes
    juju belt
    guinea eyes unfolded impossible
    squint a sun since drenched
5 breasts beaded of raised skin
    naked woman speaks
    syllables come in dust's pace
    dried, caked rim of desert mouth
    naked woman speaks
10 run mouth, tell.
    when the whites come they were dead men
    we did not want to touch them
    we did not want to interfere in their business
    after the disappearances
15 many times there were dead men among us
    and we cursed them
    and we gave them food
    when the whites came they were dead men
    five men died in our great battles before
20 guns gave us more heads of our enemies
    and those who disappeared were dead men
    and the dead take care of their own
    for things come and they leave
    enemies were dead men and whites were dead men
25 and our city and our people flourished
    and died also,

naked woman speak
syllables come in water's pace
30 long river mouth, tell.
for the skulls of our enemies
were the walls of our wealth
and we filled them with food
and palm wine for our ancestors
35 and everywhere there were skulls
white of beaten iron and guns and
white with the ancestors' praise and
white with the breath of the whites on our land
white as of eyes on sand on humid vastness
40 white as the tune of fingers, brisk on dry skin
not even pursed hungry lips were as white
and not even the sorghum was as white as this
not even the dust of the goat's grounded horn
and each night became different from the next
45 and we stood by our fires
and left the places outside our compound
to the skulls and the disappeared and the whites
and the skulls stood on their sticks
and no one was born on the nights after
50 and no one joined their age mates
the disappeared stayed away and did not
help us to kill our enemies
and we ground our breasts and our teeth to powder
55 belly roped in ashes as the sky falters on the rainbow
naked woman speaks
syllables come in palm wine's pace
run mouth, dry.

DIONNE BRAND
Trinidad and Tobago

March February Remembering

I

February blossomed
to the tramp of feet; Power
in the air.
Mandancing left his razor home
5 and marched the streets
a man among men,
Stokely's spirit marched
with the hard, hot happy crowd.

Where this march going? Mandancing
10 ask.
Thru Belmont, a brother say,
thru Woodbrook, maybe
San Juan, we might end
in Arima.
15 Leh we go, Mandancing say.

Where are the marchers of '70?

Pinkeye sits under Norville parlour;
quiet. A sad survivor.
He marched too. Like Pinetoppers,
20 like remnants of the Silkhats
gang. Like Navarrones; like
young bad brothers from Debe; like
badjohns, badmen from Belmont,
St Anns, Carrplace, John-John, Basilon; Points
25 East, Points West; brothers
marching.

In Boissiere, Boothill stands, quiet;
quiet the pacified
streets, his head
30 bad, smoke drifting in his mind, he
on soft
clouds.
The world turns,
slow, hazy,
35 a hologram; nice,
nice and warm.

Boothill march too,
thru Waterhole, thru St James
thru territory, thru turf
40 you would invade with a tank,
encompassed now with greater meaning.

II

Where this march going?
Thru cane to Caroni.
Cane blowing,
45 slow; leaf glistening
at the wedge
of sun, nicking its edges
at the breeze; leaf
like money, without memory,
50 without loyalty, without
fear; if we
stand side
by side by side, why?

Why your eyes Caneburn shinyblack
55 with fear?
Why marching's rash certainty
so clammy in your palms?

Side by Side? Remember?

The house where Pivot, New World met, was razed;
60 just mounds of twisted steel, charred wood and
blackened stone.
Points East, Points West, and north and south,
the memory of marching flares in the People's eyes.
Mandancing, Pinkeye, Boothill waiting,
65 waiting –
Waiting for the rhythms of moving feet; waiting
to move.

The world turns slowly; quiet.
The streets are nice and warm;
70 a hologram of memory; marching
side by side. Remember!

ROGER McTAIR
Trinidad and Tobago

Dreadtalk, Dub, Sermon, Prophesight and Prophesay

Kingston in the Kingdom of this World

The wind blows on the hillside
and i suffer the little children
i remember the lilies of the field
the fish swim in their shoals of silence
5 our flung nets are high wet clouds, drifting

with this reed i make music
with this pen i remember the word
with these lips i can remember the beginning of the
   world
10 between these bars is this sudden lock-up
where there is only the darkness of dog-bark
where i cannot make windmills of my hands
where i cannot run down the hill-path of faith
where i cannot suffer the little children

15 a man may have marched with armies
he may have crossed the jordan and the red sea
he may have stoned down the walls of jericho

here where the frogs creak where there is only the
   croak of starlight
20 he is reduced
he is reduced
he is reduced
         to a bundle of rags
         a broken stick
25   that will never whistle through
         fingerstops into the music of flutes
         that will never fling nets white sails
         crossing

gospel was a great wind freedom of savannas
30 gospel was a great mouth telling thunder of heroes
gospel was a cool touch warm with the sunlight like
   water in claypots, healing

this reduction wilts the flower
    weakens the water
        coarsens the lips
35 fists at the bars, shake rattle and hammers at the
    locks

suffer the little children
suffer the rose gardens
40 suffer the dark clouds howling for bread
suffer the dead fish poisoned in the lake

my authority was sunlight: the man who arose from
    the dead called me saviour
        his eyes had known moons older than jupiters
45 my authority was windmills: choirs singing of the
    flowers of rivers

your authority is these chains that strangle my wrists
your authority is the red whip that circles my head
your authority is the white eye of interrogator's terror:
50   siren price fix the law of undarkness

the dreadness of the avalanches of unjudgement

it is you who roll down boulders when I say word
it is you who cry wolf when i offer the peace of wood-
    doves
55 it is you who offer up the silence of dead leaves

i would call out but the guards do not listen
i would call out but the dew out there on the grass
    cannot glisten
i would call out but my lost children cannot unshackle
60   their shadows of silver

here i am reduced to this hole of my head
where i cannot cut wood where i cannot eat
    bread
where i cannot break fish with the multitudes

65 my authority was foot stamp upon the ground
    the curves the palms the dancers
my authority was nyambura: inching closer
        embroideries of fingers silver earrings:
            balancers

70   and

i am reduced
i am reduced
i am reduced
to these black eyes
75   this beaten face
these bleaching lips blearing obscenities

i am reduced
i am reduced
i am reduced
80   to this damp
to this dark
to this driven rag

awaiting the water of sunlight
awaiting the lilies to spring up out of the iron
85   awaiting your eyes o my little children

awaiting

EDWARD KAMAU BRATHWAITE
Barbados

Sooner or Later

Sooner or later.
But mus'.
The dam going to bus' and every man will break out
and who will stop them?
5 The force?
What force can stop this river of man
who already know their course.
The force is a centenarian. And that is far too old
one hundred years of brute force. Don't tell me dem no
     cold
'Oh' – defence force,
but dem na' defen' nott'n:
dem only come to know the ways of Babylon,
but not to partake.
15 Dem a fake.
Watch if dem don't defen' black man.
Stop them if you can.

100

The water that was used to mix the mortar for the dam
is the blood that was gathered at the slaughter of the
20   lamb.
The blood of Paul Bogle, the lamb who made them need
      the force
was used to mix the mortar for the dam that stops our
      course
25 The cement was his own black brethren who were the
      first policemen.
And when we reclaim water and cement we will run free
      again.
But sure.

30 So have-gots, have-nots,
trim-head, comb-locks, dread-knots,
is sheep from goat,
find yourself, row your own boat,
'be ready for the day'
35 it's been a long time coming,
but a change is on the way.
But how.
Sooner or later
but now –

40 right now, I and I underfed,
no clothes, no food, not even a draw to get red.
Dem want I dead?
Going dread.
Dread
45 But mus'.

BONGO JERRY
Jamaica

March 9, 1976

in a pack
dance hall
when de jump
is on
5 an' de muted
dub want to
eat itself
an de wood root
mix wid de

10 sweet scent a
ili
an de bass note
alone
stop de idrens from
15 flyin'
not a man tek
notice a de
yellow cortina
an de five wrench
20 faces inside. . .

circlin' 'roun'
a Burnin' Spear
number, machine gun
mentalities
25 centred on tripes,
everyone check
when de clappers
firs' start
dat Burnin' Spear
30 riddim gone
wil'. . .

when de fire
stop bu'n
an who nuh reach
35 groun' scale de
wall an de gully
outside, five
wrenches remain'
an' one lead
40 spattered martyr
awaitin' his medal
behin'.

down Duke st.'s
closed bound-
45 aries crew cut
accountant
ticks off a
number/closes
the doors
50 on a stars and
stripes file.

could the golf
caddy know
who fired his life
55 inspired this crime
'gainst the youth
of the town?

crying i sight
brown grass
60 of a city
trying to out
dry flames
with i tears.

BRIAN MEEKS
Jamaica

The Road of the Dread

That dey road no pave
like any other black-face road
it no have no definite colour
and it fence two side
5   with live barbwire.

And no look fi no milepost
fi measure you walking
and no tek no stone as
dead or familiar

10 for sometime you pass a ting
you know as . . . call it stone again
and is a snake ready fi squeeze yu
kill yu
or is a dead man tek him
15 possessions tease yu
Then the place dem yu feel
is resting place because time
before that yu welcome like rain,
go dey again?
20 bad dawg, bad face tun fi drive yu underground
wey yu no have no light fi walk
and yu find sey that many yu meet who sey
them understand
is only from dem mout dem talk.

25 One good ting though, that same treatment
    mek yu walk untold distance
    for to continue yu have fe walk far
    away from the wicked.

    Pan dis same road ya sista
30 sometime yu drink yu salt sweat fi water
    for yu sure sey at least dat no pisen,
    and bread? yu picture it and chew it accordingly
    and some time yu surprise fi know how dat full
    man belly.

35 Some day no have no definite colour
    no beginning and no ending, it just name day
    or night as how you feel fi call it.

    Den why I tread it brother?
    well mek I tell yu bout the day dem
40 when the father send some little bird
    that swallow flute fi trill me
    And when him instruct the sun fi smile pan me first.

    and the sky calm like sea when it sleep
    and a breeze like a laugh follow mi.
45 or the man find a stream that pure like baby mind
    and the water ease down yu throat
    and quiet yu inside.

    and better still when yu meet another traveller
    who have flour and yu have water and man and man
50 make bread together.
    And dem time dey the road run straight and sure
    like a young horse that cant tire
    and yu catch a glimpse of the end
    through the water in yu eye
55 I wont tell yu what I spy
    but is fi dat alone I tread this road.

LORNA GOODISON
Jamaica

Apocalypse Dub

At first, there's a thin, bright Rider –
he doesn't stop at the supermarket, the cool
red meats are not to his taste.
He steals from the tin on the tenement table,
5 he munches seed from the land
where no rain has fallen, he feeds
in the gutter behind my house.
The bread is covered with sores
when he eats it; the children
10 have painted his face on their bellies

The second rides slowly, is visiting, watch him, he smiles
through the holes in the roof
of the cardboard houses.
His exhaust sprays pus on the sheets,
15 he touches the women and teaches them
fever, he puts eggs under the skin –
in the hot days insects will hatch and hide
in the old men's mouths,
in the bones of the children

20 And always, behind them, the iceman, quick,
with his shades, the calm oil of his eyes –
when he throttles, the engine
grunts like a killer. I'm afraid,
you said. Then you closed the window
25 and turned up the radio, the DJ said greetings
to all you lovely people.
But in the street the children coughed like guns.

In the blueblack evenings
they cruise on the corner
30 giggling. Skenneng! Skenneng!

DENNIS SCOTT
Jamaica

The Dispatcher

Jack Spratt

wake up feeling alright
after business last night
conduct satisfactory
5 his hand full a ring
and other ting
cant mention in public
like gun and blood dunny

his grannie
10 did beat him
with supple jack cant done
boy so tough
never cry
Grannie say
15 is bad seed

Jack Spratt come to town
to make something of life
country boy dont know nothing
but hoe, learn so fast
20 bout contracting
move so high is Jack Spratt
control territory
three police and a
half-Chiney beas
25 that is secretary to big man in town
(have a wife that ripe
for the plucking like mango
or naseberry. . . . . .)

Jack Spratt look so right
30 kareeba and shades
well spoken and bright
drive BMW in daytime
Toyota at night
flashing cheque book
35 and passport all visaed
to go, have a room
in the ghetto, apartment
on hillside where his neighbour
is first cousin to a Minister's wife

40 (She complain bout his stereo
but shut up when Jack Spratt
just sight her. Say
she sorry. He is perfectly
right to make noise
45 in the territory.
Is not true that she nervous bout him
and his idren but she leaving tomorrow
moving in with a friend.)

Jack Spratt call himself
50 many things. Public Servant.
Contractor. People who say
overpopulation is the greatest
curse of the nation should
give medal to Jack Spratt
55 for what we over-produce
Jack Spratt will reduce
with efficiency and dispatch.

Jack Spratt dispatch
thirteen. Police hold him
60 three time but not long.
In this country Jack Spratt
walk bout free for he have
the connection Jack Spratt
have ability Jack Spratt
65 have mobility have contacts
and contracts Jack Spratt
have the might and the right
to decide who sleeping
in tonight and who outside
70 in Hope River bottom
or in cold Sandy Gully.

How Jack Spratt fly
so high? Stay up there
so long? Jack Spratt see.
75 Jack Spratt know.
Jack Spratt nuh John Crow?

OLIVE SENIOR
Jamaica

Language Barrier

Jamaica language sweet yuh know bwoy,
An yuh know mi nebba notice i',
Till tarra day one foreign frien'
Come spen some time wid mi.

5 An den im call mi attention to
Some tings im sey soun' queer,
Like de way wi always sey 'koo yah'
When we really mean 'look here'.

Den annodda ting whey puzzle im,
10 Is how wi lub 'repeat' wise' 'f
For de ongle time im repeat a wud
Is when smaddy half deaf.

Todda day im a walk outa road
An when im a pass one gate,
15 Im see one bwoy a one winda,
An one nodda one outside a wait.

Im sey dem did look kine o' nice
Soh im ben a go sey howdy,
But im tap shart when de fus' bwoy sey
20 'A ready yuh ready aready?'

Den like sey dat ney quite enuff,
Fe po' likkle foreign Hugh,
Him hear de nedda bwoy halla out,
'A come mi come fe come wait fe yuh'.

25 An dat is nat all dat puzzle him,
Why wi run wi words togedda?
For when im expec' fe hear 'the other',
Him hear dis one word, 'todda'.

Instead o' wi sey 'all of you'
30 Wi ongle sey unoo,
Him can dis remember sey
De wud fe 'screech owl' is 'patoo'.

As fe some expression him hear,
Im wouldn badda try meck dem out,
35 Like 'boonoonoonoos ' 'chamba-chamba',
An 'kibba up yuh mout'.

Him can hardly see de connection,
Between 'only' an 'dengey',
An im woulda like fe meet de smaddy
40 Who invent de wud 'preckey'.

Mi advise im no fe fret imself,
For de Spaniards do it to,
For when dem mean fe sey 'jackass',
Dem always sey 'burro'.

45 De French, Italian, Greek an Dutch,
Dem all guilty o' de crime
None a dem no chat im language,
Soh Hugh betta larn fe mime.

But sayin' dis an dat yuh know,
50 Some o' wi cyan eben undastan one anodda,
Eben doah wi all lib yah
An chat de same patois.

For from las' week mi a puzzle out,
Whey Joey coulda mean,
55 When im teck im facey self soh ax
Ef any o' im undapants clean.

VALERIE BLOOM
Jamaica

Listen Mr Oxford Don

Me not no Oxford don
me a simple immigrant
from Clapham Common
I didn't graduate
5 I immigrate

But listen Mr Oxford don
I'm a man on de run
and a man on de run
is a dangerous one

10 I ent have no gun
I ent have no knife
but mugging de Queen's English
is the story of my life

I dont need no axe
15 to split/ up yu syntax
I dont need no hammer
to mash up yu grammar

I warning you Mr Oxford don
I'm a wanted man
20 and a wanted man
is a dangerous one

Dem accuse me of assault
on de Oxford dictionary/
imagin a concise peaceful man like me/
25 dem want me serve time
for inciting rhyme to riot
but I tekking it quiet
down here in Clapham Common

I'm not a violent man Mr Oxford don
30 I only armed wit muh human breath
but human breath
is a dangerous weapon

So mek dem send one big word after me
I ent serving no jail sentence
35 I slashing suffix in self-defence
I bashing future wit present tense
and if necessary

I making de Queen's English accessory/to my offence

JOHN AGARD
Jamaica

Inglan is a Bitch

w'en mi jus' come to Landan toun
mi use to work pan di andahgroun
but workin' pan di andahgroun
y'u don't get fi know your way aroun'

5 Inglan is a bitch
dere's no escapin' it
Inglan is a bitch
dere's no runnin' whey fram it

mi get a lickle jab in a big 'otell
10 an' awftah a while, mi woz doin' quite well
dem staat mi aaf as a dish–washah
but w'en mi tek a stack, mi noh tun clack–watchah!

Inglan is a bitch
dere's no escapin it
15 Inglan is a bitch
noh baddah try fi hide fram it

w'en dem gi' you di lickle wage packit
fus dem rab it wid dem big tax rackit
y'u haffi struggle fi mek en's meet
20 an' w'en y'u goh a y'u bed y'u jus' cant sleep

Inglan is a bitch
dere's no escapin it
Inglan is a bitch fi true
a noh lie mi a tell, a true

25 mi use to work dig ditch w'en it cowl noh bitch
mi did strang like a mule, but, bwoy, mi did fool
den awftah a while mi jus' stap dhu ovahtime
den aftah a while mi jus' phu dung mi tool

Inglan is a bitch
30 dere's no escapin it
Inglan is a bitch
y'u haffi know how fi suvvive in it

well mi dhu day wok an' mid dhu nite wok
mi dhu clean wok an' mid dhu dutty wok
35 dem seh dat black man is very lazy
but if y'u si how mi wok y'u woulda sey mi crazy

Inglan is a bitch
dere's no escapin it
Inglan is a bitch
40 y'u bettah face up to it

dem have a lickle facktri up inna Brackly
inna disya facktri all dem dhu is pack crackry
fi di laas fifteen years dem get mi laybah
now awftah fiteen years mi fall out a fayvah

45 Inglan is a bitch
   dere's no escapin it
   Inglan is a bitch
   dere's no runnin' whey fram it

   mi know dem have work, work in abundant
50 yet still, dem mek mi redundant
   now, at fifty–five mi gettin' quite ol'
   yet still, dem sen' mi fi goh draw dole

   Inglan is a bitch
   dere's no escapin it
55 Inglan is a bitch fi true
   is whey wi a goh dhu 'bout it?

LINTON KWESI JOHNSON
Jamaica

Echo

      fi i de ghetto youth
      it kinda cute
      all day i trod earth
      a look fi work
   5 till i shoes sole wear down
      an i foot a touch de groun
      wey i live fa   eh?
      a nu sey i nu have nu faith
      but dis ya sufferation ya
   10 a whole heapa weight
      sufferin unda dis ya sun
      i a tell yu is nu fun
      curfew
      baton lick
   15 tear gas
      gun shat
      jail
      no bail
      dats de lot i haffi bear
   20 fi i de ghetto youth
      it kinda cute
      trod earth
      look fi work
      shoes sole wear down

112

25 foot a touch di groun
   wey I a live fa   eh!
   a nu sey i nu have nu faith
   but dis ya sufferation ya
   a whole heapa weight.

OKU ONUORA
Jamaica

Still Deh Deh

   ole ooman
   han strech out
   a beg inna di sun
   a bun inna di
5 rain
   pain a lick
   yu
   bone a click
   click
10 dem tek a
   fotografe a yu
   win a prize
   as bes human intres
   pikcha
15   an yu still deh
   pon di caana
   a beg
   ole ooman
   a bun
20   dem talk a speech
   bout yu
   get a standin ovation
   as most concern
   politician
25   an yu still deh deh
   pon di caana
   a batta
   ole ooman
   dem shoot a flim pon yu
30   an yu still deh deh
   dem ak a play pon yu
     an yu still deh deh

dem journalize pon yu
  an yu still deh deh
35 inna di sun
   inna di rain
   a beg
   a bun
   a suffa
40 ole ooman. . . .
   dem write a poetry
   bout yu

MBALA
Jamaica

Talkin' Blues

   Yeah oh yeah
   Cold ground was my bed last night
   and rock was my pillow too
   Cold ground was my bed last night
5 and rock was my pillow too
   I'm saying talkin blues, talkin blues
   They say your feet is just too big for
       your shoes
   Talkin blues, talkin blues `
10 Your feet is just too big for your shoes

   I've been down on the rock for so long
   I seem to wear a permanent screw
   I've been down on the rock for so long
   I seem to wear a permanent screw
15 But I'm gonna stare in the sun,
   let the rays shine in my eyes
   I'm gonna take a just a one step more
   Cause I feel like bombing a church
   Now that you know that the preacher
20   is lying
   So who's gonna stay at home
   When the freedom fighters are fighting
   Talkin blues, talkin blues
   They say your feet is just too big for
25   your shoes
   Talkin blues, keep on talkin blues
   They say, you hear what they say, didn't
       you hear

Cold ground was my bed last night
30 rockstone was my pillow too
Cold ground was my bed last night
and rock was my pillow too
Talkin' blues, talkin' blues
I seem to wear a permanent screw.

BOB MARLEY
Jamaica

Rat Race

Ah! Ya too rude
Oh what a rat race
Oh what a rat race
This is the rat race

5 Some a lawful, some a bastard
Some a jacket
Oh what a rat race, rat race

Some a gorgan, some a hooligan
Some a guine-gog
10 In this rat race, yeah!
Rat race
I'm singing
When the cats away
The mice will play
15 Political violence fill ya city
Yea-ah!
Don't involve Rasta in your say
say
Rasta don't work for no CIA
20 Rat race, Rat race, Rat race
When you think is peace and safety
A sudden destruction
Collective security for surety
Yeah!
25 Don't forget your history
Know your destiny
In the abundance of water
The fool is thirsty
Rat race, Rat race, Rat race

Oh it's a disgrace to see the
   Human race in a rat race, rat race
   You got the horse race
   You got the human race
35 But this is a rat race, rat race.

BOB MARLEY
Jamaica

Butta Pan Kulcha

   a me one
   a travel de lan
   wid mi likkle butta pan.
   dem nuh andastan.
5 a me one
   jus a travel de lan
   wid mi likkle dutty pan
   dem nuh andastan.

   mi walk de lane
10 inna sun and rain
   mi nuh feel nuh pain
   mi nuh ave nuh shame.

   a jus me one
   just a travel de lan
15 wid mi likkle butta pan
   dem nuh andastan.

   mi family lef fe heaven lass year
   and society seh dem nuh care.
   dem seh mi mad
20 mi feel bad
   mi nuh ave nuh fren
   nuh money fi spen.

   a mi one
   wid mi likkle dutty pan
25 dem nuh andastan.

   mi cook inna it
   den use it meck pit
   mi nuh ave nuh bed
   fi lay mi head

30   a jus me one
     jus a travel de lan
     wid me likkle butta pan
     dem nuh andastan!

     and society seh dem nuh care
35   or maybe is through dem
     don't aware
     dat a man like me
     still tryin to be free
     from dis misery.

40   a me one
     wid mi likkle butta pan
     just a travel de lan
     dem nuh andastan.

     Dem pass mi pon de street
45   and hiss dem teeth
     but mi laugh inna mi mind
     cause a nuh mi commit de crime

     a jus me one
     wid mi likkle butta pan
50   dem nuh andastan.

     an' is just time
     an' dem wi si
     dat nat me create de society
54   and meck it stink. . . . .

              MUTABARUKA
               Jamaica

Trainer

     Yuh tink a little bit a tings me go through, Trainer?
     I use to live inna one yard which part
     everybody tink dem better off dan de odder,
     and de only ting me coulda do
5   fi meck dem know dat me naw skin-up
     when de area ready fi go erupt
     is fi meck dem know
     dat me is a man dat will bun up harp
     an tear off house-top, because
10 I got some wicked thoughts.

Me a tell you, Trainer,
dat I pass some man pon corner
dat I know a some ole murderer.
An see I ya? I still deh ya!

15 Dat one night
a just get up.
for a did feel fed-up,
and flash de area.

A teck a walk come up ya,
20 dat when yuh teck a stock
is a dance a en up at.
Dance crash. An a ready fi tracks
but las bus stop.
A never have no taxi fare,
25 plus a jus never did live anywhere.
So a just walk
an hold me head in de air.

A naw tell no lie.
Just as a reach de square
30 a hear a man seh,
'Kiss me ass! A goin help yuh
fi reach home before it dark!'
An im grab one little bwoy inna im wais
an before de little bwoy coulda open im mout
35 im seh, 'A who give you permission fi talk?
How ole yuh is
fi a stay outa yuh yard till after dark?'
De bwoy seh, 'Me? Me a fourteen, sah.'
An de man dash on de cat-a-nine,
40 an im bawl out, 'Lawd Jesus Christ!
Me a twenty-nine!'

Me couldn tell im dat me no live nowhere!
So me pull a skank despite im rank.
By dis time a three day me no sleep
45 an God bless wha me eat.

A beg a piece of newspaper
and a head fi de public house
dat dem seh renk an full a crab-louse,
dat when a reach deh
50 a just satta an fall asleep
because I did feel well weak.

Yuy know what wake me up, Trainer?
Is a man come deh inna de early morning.
Im mus did know is a human
55 siddung deh a ketch a nap,
yet im dash a bucket a Jeyes water pon me
widout even saying sorry at dat.
A look pon im. A never seh one ting.
For yuh know how a did feel, Trainer?
60 Fi kill im!

A teck out me ice-pick an a grab im.
An same time a hear someting seh, 'No jook im!'
An anodder ting seh,
'Jook im inna im neck meck him run an fret!'
65 An a see a whole heap a blood
jus a circle roun im. An a let im go,
siddung, an laugh. 'But look pon you, to rass!'

Same time a man come on an seh, 'Get up!
Yuh doan see dat dis-ya place ya dutty-up?'
70 An a look pon im, an a never seh one ting

for it was de firs time in me life
a really feel fi seh something
an a couldn bring out nuttin

so a just walk.

MICHAEL SMITH
Jamaica

Instant Ting
For Michael Smith

Was an instant ting
When ah sight im
Was an instant ting
When ah sight im

5 Swift as ah hawk
With ah hop an drop walk
Limber like ah whip
For ah hop an drop lick
An im face lookin grim

119

10 Like im out pon a limb
Was an instant ting
When ah sight im

Im cut a picture
Of trouble in store
15 Im look familiar
To de days of yore
Was an instant ting
When ah sight im

Was an instant ting
20 When ah hear im
Was an instant ting
'S-a-y-y Nattie Nattie
doe Baddar dash way yo culture'

25 Swift as ah hawk
With an hop an drop walk
Limber like ah whip
For ah hop an drop lick
An im face looking grim
30 Like im out pon a limb
Was an instant ting
When ah hear im

Im paint a picture
Of trouble in store
35 Im sound familiar
To de days of yore
Was an instant ting
When ah hear im

Was an instant ting
40 When dem sight im
Was an instant ting
When dem sight im
'– Babylon to mih right
Babylon to mih left
45 Babylon in front of I
and Babylon behind I
and I an I alone
Like ah Goliath
wid ah sling shot –'

50 Swift as ah hawk
With ah hop an drop walk
Limber like ah whip
For ah hop an drop lick
An im face lookin grim
55 Like im out pon ah limb
Was an instant ting
When dem sight im

Im cut ah picture
Of trouble in store
60 Im look familiar
To de days of yore
Was an instant ting
When dem sight im

Was an instant ting
65 When dem hear im
Was an instant ting
When dem hear im
'I MAN FREE TO WALK ANY PART OF JAMAICA'

Swift as ah hawk
70 With ah hop an drop walk
Stinging like ah whip
With ah hop an drop lick
An im face looking grim
Like im out pon ah limb
75 Was an instant ting
When dem hear im

Im paint ah picture
Of trouble in store
Im sound familiar
80 To de days of yore
Was an instant ting
When dem hear im

Was an instant ting
When dem stone im
85 Was an instant ting
When dem stone im
It paint ah picture
Of trouble in store
It look familiar
90 To de days of yore

For de words of Jah say
'Touch not the Lord's annointed
And do his prophets no harm'
And the voice of the whirlwind say –
95 S-E E E E E
A-A A A A
G A
Was an instant ting
When dem kill im
100 Was an instant ting
When dem kill im

DELANO ABDUL MALIK DECOTEAU
Grenada

Mama Dot Warns Against an Easter Rising

Doan raise no kite is good friday
but is out he went out an fly it
us thinkin maybe dere wont be a breeze
strong enouf an widout any a we to hole it
5 fo him he'd neva manage to get it high up
to de tree top ware de wind kissin
de ripess sweetess fruit we cawn reach
but he let out some string bit by bit
tuggin de face into de breeze
10 coaxin it up all de time taking a few steps back
and it did rise up bit by bit till de lang tail
din't touch de groun an we grip de palin
we head squeeze between to watch him
an trace its rise rise rise up up up in de sky
15 we all want to fly in like bird but can only kite
fly an he step back juss as we beginnin
to smile fo him envy him his easter risin
when bap he let out a scream leggo string
an de kite drop outta de sky like a bird
20 a sail down to de nex field an we runnin to him
forgetting de kite we uncle dem mek days ago
fram wood shave light as bird bone
paper tin like fedder an de tongue o kite
fo singin in de sky like a bird an de tail
25 fo balance string in de mout like it pullin
de longess worm an he a hole him foot
an a bawl we could see seven inch a greenhart

gone in at de heel runnin up him leg
like a vein he groanin all de way to de haspital
30 on de cross-bar a bike ridden by a uncle
she not sayin a word but we hearin her
fo de ress a dat day an evry year since
doan raise no kite is good friday
an de sky was a birdless kiteless wait fo her word

FRED D'AGUIAR
Guyana

Calypso

Graf Zeppelin

One Sunday morning I chanced to hear
A rumbling and a tumbling in the atmosphere } *(repeat)*
I ran to stare, people were flocking everywhere
Gesticulating, gazing, and pointing in the air
5 It was the Graf Zeppelin which had
Come to pay a visit to Trinidad

I gazed at the Zeppelin contemplatively
And marvelled at man's ingenuity
The whirring of the engine was all I heard
10 As it floated in the air like some giant bird
And in between, as the mighty airship leaned
The pilot and sailors and passengers were seen
They were waving little flags they had
Heralding their visit to Trinidad

15 I gazed and the knowledge came back to me
How wonderful the work of man could be
To see that huge object in the air
Maintaining perfect equilibrium in the atmosphere
Wonderfully, beautifully, gloriously
20 Decidedly defying all the laws of gravity
Was the Graf Zeppelin which had
Come to pay a visit to Trinidad

As I gazed at the Zeppelin something touched my hand
I turned and saw an old decrepit Indian man
25 He said to me pointing at the Zeppelin
Massa, can you tell me what is that thing?
Me feel to bawl, for me no understand at all,
He no have nothing hold him up dey, but still he never
fall
He was speaking of the Zeppelin that had
30 Come to pay a visit to Trinidad

The visit of the Zeppelin will ever be
Indelibly impressed in my memory

Such a sight I'd never seen before
I gazed at it in consternation and awe
35 I chanced to hear, a big fat woman said Me dear
Not for a million dollars I would't go up in the air
They may talk about modernity
But I think that the ground good enough for me.

ATILLA THE HUN (Raymond Quevedo)
Trinidad and Tobago

The Gold in Africa

The Gold, the gold
The Gold, the gold
The gold in Africa
Mussolini want from the Emperor

5 Abyssinia appeal to the League for peace
Mussolini actions were like a beast,
A villain, a thief, a highway robber
And a shameless dog for a dictator

He crossed the border and added (?) more
10 The Emperor had no intentions for war
That man I call a criminal
The man destroyed churches and hospitals

He said expansion he really need
He had forty-five million heads to feed
15 Why he don't attack the Japanese
England, France, or hang on to Germany?

The man want to kill King Haile Selassie
To enslave his territory
They began to cry for food and water
20 In that burning desert of Africa

We have diamond ruby and pearl
Platinum, silver and even gold
Ah don't know why the man making so much strife
I now believe he want Haile Selassie wife

If he want gold as a dictator
      Try in Demerara
      Venezuela or Canada
      Austro-Hungar (y) or else in America

TIGER (Neville Marcano)
Trinidad and Tobago

Take Your Meat Out Me Rice

I
A Bajan and a Trinidadian
Dying with starvation
The Bajan say 'Look,
Trini, leh we make a cook.
5 Oi put de rice, you going put de meat,
The we goin both have something to eat.'
Now when the pot was nearly to done
The Bajan decide to pull a fast one.

He seh, 'Trini, I'm a born Barbadian
10 Ah don' like to foight
But when come to de occasion
Man, ah stick for mih right
You put in a twelve-cents meat bone
You worse than a lice
15 Oi goin' give you a word of advice
Tyeck yo' meat out mih roice.'

II
Trini got in a big rage
'Whu wrong wid you Baije?
Ah got tell you flat,
20 Baije, I ehn taking that!
When we was shipping we both agree
The food will be cooked and shared equally
Ah put mih last penny in this meat
And I ain't movin until ah eat.'

25 Baije say, 'Trini, I'm a born Barbadian
Ah don' like to foight
But when come to de occasion
Man, ah die for mih right.
You put in a ten-cents meat bone

30   You think that is noice?
      Well don't make me have to tell you twice
      Tyeck yo' meat out mih roice.'

      III
      The Bajan then say to Trini,
      'Man, doh tell lies pun me
35   I never told you
      That we go join and cook up in two.
      What I mention oi can repeat:
      I said to lend me a piece o' meat.'
      Trini so vex, he began to cry
40   'Baije, in front mih eye you telling a lie'.

      Baije seh, 'Trini' I'm a born Barbadian
      I don't like to fight
      But when come to the occasion
      Man, ah die for mih right
45   You put in a nine-cents meat bone
      Good Lawd! You want half a slice!
      If you don't want to pay the price
      Take you' meat out mih rice.'

      IV
      By this time the pot finish
50   Trini pick up a dish
      The Bajan say, 'Now! Now! Now!
      It never happen so!
      If you wanted something to eat,
      Man, take a fork and dig out you' meat
55   But if you have one gram o' rice
      B' Chrisse! Ah Ah squeeze you throat like a vice.'

      'Trini! I'm a born Barbadian
      I don' like to fight
      But when I come to the occasion,
60   Man, I die for mih right
      You put in a eight-cents meat bone
      You Trinidian loice
      Before ah squeeze you like Chrois'
      Take your meat out mih rice.'

                  LORD KITCHENER (Aldwyn Roberts)
                       Trinidad and Tobago

Fountain of Youth

I
Suppose it happen in truth
Something spring up call the Fountain of Youth
If it on a mountain peak in the sky
People going for a bath don't care if they die
5 Just imagine a man a hundred years old
See him how he climbing a greasy pole
You could be old as any King Kong
As you take the bath you coming back young

Chorus
Then, see mih great grandfather playing hopscotch and
10   pitching marble
And mih great grandmother with a hula hoop making trouble
The old people today in town
You could hear them talking 'bout when they was young
But with the fountain they will be bold
15 The whole talk go' change to when they was old

II
Ol' people today who know that they ol'
Never had a chance to dance rock'n roll
With the fountain, yes it will be hell
They will be supple like the snake they call macajuel
20 Those ol' women they go to get the crake (?)
To put on they tight dress to walk and shake
All o' dem who canary cover tun dung
Hell and high water when they come back young

Chorus (As above)

III
Believe it or not I'll mention mih name:
25 The Spoiler. To tell you this I ain't shame
A done ole me old as you all can see
And not a women in the world ain' meddle with me
Ah heard that they say the Russians dem soon
Decide to send man up to the moon
30 So if is up there the fountain explo'
Bet you life I'se the first man that want to go

Chorus
And then, see the Spoiler having women like he have – chickens
I'll be young again so to me there will be some easy – pickings
I'll be walking about the place
35 Getting women with mih youthful face

I'll be flying like an aeroplane
Because ah come back young, ah ain' ol' again.

IV
Suppose it happen. I mean, so to speak
You have to renew the bath once a week
40 Poor you, you ain' know you taking a stroll
With a woman 'bout a hundred and three years old
She ain' renew she bath: you making you' love
Talking 'bout de moon and de stars above
An when you hear the shout, now whe you go do?
45 She face turn like a salt prunes in front o you

Oh Lord! You want to dead when you look at what you was –
kissing
Yes you cannot move cause you foot and dem they ain't – moving
And you trembling like a leaf
50 Can't get away from the young old beef
And she telling you kiss she, don't be afraid
Is forget she forget to renew she bathe.

SPOILER (Theophilus Phillip)
Trinidad and Tobago

Dan is the Man

I
According to the education you get when you small
You'll grow up with true ambition and respect from one an all
But in my days in school they teach me like a fool
The things they teach me I should be a block-headed mule.

5 Pussy has finished his work long ago
And now he resting and thing
Solomon Agundy was born on a Monday
The Ass in the Lion skin
Winkin Blinkin and Nod
10 Sail off in a wooden shoe
How the Agouti lose he tail and Alligator trying to get
monkey liver soup.

II
The poems and the lessons they write and send from England
Impress me they were trying to cultivate comedians
15 Comic books made more sense

You know it was fictitious without pretence
But like Cutteridge wanted to keep us in ignorance.

Humpty Dumpty sat on a wall
Humpty Dumpty did fall
20   Goosey Goosey Gander
Where shall I wander
Ding dong dell . . . Pussy in the well
RIKKI . . . TIKKI TAVI.
Rikki Tikki Tavi

III
25   Well Cutteridge he was plenty times more advanced than
     them scientists
I ain't believe that no one man could write so much foolishness
Aeroplane and rockets didn't come too soon
Scientist used to make the grade in balloon
30   This time Cutteridge done make a cow jump over the moon.

Tom Tom the piper son
Stole the pig and away he ran
Once there was a woman who lived in a shoe
She had so many children she didn't know what to do
35   Dickery Dickery Dock
The mouse run up the Clock
The lion and the mouse
A woman pushing a cow up a ladder to eat grass on top a house.

IV
How I happen to get some education my friends I don't know
40   All they teach me is about Brer Rabbit and Rumplestilskin. . .O
They wanted to keep me down indeed
They tried their best but didn't succeed
You see I was dunce and up to now I can't read.

Peter Peter was a pumpkin eater
45   And the Lilliput people tie Gulliver
When I was sick and lay abed
I had two pillows at my head
I see the Goose that lay the golden egg
The Spider and the Fly
Morocoy with wings flying in the sky
50   They beat me like a dog to learn that in school
If me head was bright I woulda be a damn fool.

SPARROW (Slinger Francisco)
Grenada

Dis Place Nice

I
You talk about a place where the people have carefree living!
This is such a place of fun-loving spreeing and fete-in
Dis the land where people don't care if Ash Wednesday fall on
           Good Friday
5 Man they love to struggle in this happy go-lucky way.
It's blockerama, feterama, and just now it's massorama.

So the foreigner come for Carnival
And he telling heself after he had a ball
Trinidad is nice Trinidad is a paradise
10 Mr Foreigner, in La Trinity
The people have a carnival mentality
Trinidad is nice, Trinidad is a paradise
They are not serious, very few conscious
So I cannot agree with my own chorus
15 Trinidad is nice, Trinidad is a paradise
But ah hear some people talking about revolution day,
Change is on the way.

II
They born in a land the better part controlled by the aliens
They fill the pockets of Portuguese, Chinese and Syrians,
20 Trinidadians is who should own land;
Now is the time to make the land their possession
But their sense of taste could just trace
To all them fancy show-case
So the businessman, he blow their mind
25 And his dollars they got to find.

Trinidad is nice for men like Sabga
Kirpalani, Maharaj an Y de Lima
Trinidad is nice, Trinidad is a paradise
Business expanding, more bank they building
30 So is the capitalists and them who should sing
Trinidad is nice, Trinidad is a paradise
And like the slave masters want to bring back the whip
But ah hear mih sister talking about revolution day
Fire on the way.

III
35 They don't know their worth; like they haven't a sense of value
They don't know their rights; even that they cannot argue
Three quarter of a million people

131

Cannot get up and do something about the struggle
But they plan for the next holiday
40 To fete their lives away
Forgetting that they own the soil
On which their foreparents toil.

For the people who form the constitution laws
For the oppressors and foreign investors
45 Trinidad is nice, Trinidad is a paradise
Amoco and Shell business doing swell
On your oil them foreign parasites dwell
Trinidad is nice, Trinidad is a paradise
Yet the song I sing, is like I hearing
The chorus singing 'God Save the King'
50 Trinidad is nice, Trinidad is a paradise
But ah hear my brother talking about revolution day
Fighting on the way.

VALENTINO (Emerold Phillip)
Trinidad and Tobago

Bassman

I
Ah was planning to forget
calypso
And go and plant peas in
Tobago,
5 But I am afraid,
Ah can't make the grade,
Cause every night I lie down
in my bed,
Ah hearing a bassman in meh
10 head.
Poom poom poom poom
poom etc

Chorus
Ah don't know how this thing
get inside me.
15 But every morning he driving
me crazy

Like he taking meh head for a
　　panyard,
Morning and evening,
20　Like this fella gone mad,
Tim Tom – if ah don't want to
　　sing,
Tim tom – when he start to do
　　he ting
25　Ah don't want to but I have
　　to sing
Tim Tom – if ah don't want
　　to dance
Tim Tom – he does have me in
30　a trance,
Ah don't want to but I have to
　　prance.

II
One night I said to the bassman,
35　Give me your identification,
He said is me Farell,
Your bassman from hell,
They tell me you singing
　　calypso,
40　And ah come to pull some
　　notes for you,
Poom poom poom poom
　　poom etc

Chorus

III
Ah went and ah tell Dr Leon,
45　I want ah brain operation,
Ah man in meh head ah want
　　him to dead
He said it's my imagination,
But I know ah hearing the
50　bassman,
Poom poom poom poom
　　poom etc

Chorus

MIGHTY SHADOW (Winston Bailey)
Trinidad and Tobago

Deaf Pan Men

I

Big Propaganda
They say this year have no Panorama*
Pan men getting deaf
Some in the right and some in the left
5 Somebody say the pan men gone deaf fo' true
It's now calypsonians are turning blue
They put calypsonians tunes on the shelf
Pan men say they playing their Mas by they self

Chorus
Ring ting ping pong, ping pong
10 Steelbands going to wail in town
They sounding sweet, they sounding sweet
Masquerade on Frederick Street
Some playing B flat, some playing F
They can't hear a thing because they deaf
15 But they going to jam
And the name of the Mas' is Dr Williams
An hope you understand the masquerade
Pan men in dark shade wearing hearing aid.

II

Like Lord Kitchener
20 I out o' the Road March business this year
I say so because
I know Kitchener get some inside scores
Is no use we making tunes for the Pan
The Pan Men can't hear they can't understand
25 Is better we join up the free-for-all
And Jour'vert morning line up up by Whitehall

Chorus: first and last four lines the same
Some playing in G some playing C
Some are even playing GCE

III

Dr Williams say
30 He leading the band from early Jou'vert
Now he made me to understand
He only want deaf people inside the band

He say that he's heading the big parade
Supplying every Pan Man with hearing aid
35 So I bound to be in the Savannah
To witness deaf Pan Men Panorama

    Chorus: first and last four lines the same
    Some playing in C, some lost their key
    Some are very near to WC

IV
Paul Getty Junior
40 Grandson of the world famous millionaire
He could hardly hear
Since the kidnappers chop off his ear
Ah hear that he sent down a telegram
Stating that he coming to knock some pan
45 He say he got credentials to make the grade
We only have to supply him with hearing aid

    Chorus: first and last four lines the same
    Some playing 'cello, some playing bass
    Some of them are really playing the(ir) mass.

              RELATOR (William Harris)
              Trinidad and Tobago

* ***Panorama:*** Steelband competition

The Devil

I
So you 'fraid Satan
That mysterious man
And you keep saying
In hell he living
5 Is time you know
You thinking wrong
Devils for so
All over town

Chorus
You fraid de devil
10 You fraid him bad

135

Well look de devil
Right in yuh yard
And he grinnin' while you saying grace
Shaking up e tail in people face
15 Whe de devil dey
Whe de devil dey
Look de devil dey

II
To fool people eyes
Devil does disguise
20 But is no problem
To recognise them
Some like to deck
In suit whole day
And round their neck
25 A balisier*

Chorus (as before)

III
It have some devil
With gown and bible
Who praise their saviour
But cuss their neighbour
30 Another kind
Share kicks and blows
Hiding behind
Some police clothes

Chorus (as before)

IV
Devils in business
35 In halls of justice
In pot-guts old men
Who seduce girl children
And if you praise
And if you praise
40 The wrongs men do
Well then you is
A devil too

Chorus (as before)

PENGUIN (Sedley Joseph)
Trinidad and Tobago

* **Balisier:** Heliconia flower, symbol of the then ruling People's Natio
Movement in Trinidad

Apocalypse

I
Last night, while I was trying to rest mih head
A vision appeared to me as I was lying in mih bed
Four riders; each one had a different horse
They say they going down Caroni, they want to check out the
5   new race course
Ministers, businessmen, even a president
Kneel down worshipping these horse as if it was the day of
                                           judgement
Though he was present, they ignored the Son of Man
10 Because like to worship a horse was their religion
So ah turned and ah asked what all this signify
And everthing was revealed to me by the Most High

Ah see a horse laughing kee, kee, kee
He say he have connections in a big political party
15 'Guess which party', was what the horse say
But then ah notice he tail was a balisier

II
And the first white horse was vibrant and strong
And the rider had a bow, and on his head was a crown
And it unfolded to me that this is how horseracing should be
20 It is a sport of kings, and its fraternity
But of my government, look whu you do!
Take so much from so many to give to so few
You are sadly lacking in your priority
Affording so much money to a Racing Authority.
25 And every Sunday morning I watching TV for house in lottery
Like you consider this beast of burden before me

Ah see a horse laughing kee, kee, kee
He say in this country is he spending we money
He say that if wishes were horses beggars would ride
So the Complex is for beggars to ride and fall and break their
30   backside

III
Behold a second horse, like unto the first
But this one was red signifying that things really getting worse
When corrupt men get position in any society
35 See how clear this is reflected by my Racing Authority
A ex-minister involved in the Tri-Star racket
But when you see him racing day, he dress up in tie and jacket
An' a certain minister who use to work Texaco

Building a big palace down in South, where he get money
40 nobody know
And the rider of this horse had a sword in e hand
Forever handing out disrespect to the poor man

Ah see a horse laughing kee, kee, kee
Boasting that he sure he have a better house than me
45 He say from the beginning the horse come before the buggy
So build a home for the horse, and leave the people in box-board
shanty

IV
Behold a third rider with a scale in hand
Signifying even more suffering for the poor man
50 The scale means a shortage in materials and labour
More difficulty for poor people to get shelter
What about teachers? What about the Judiciary?
And what about we ailing record industry?
You insult the whole Tobago Assembly
55 Two-forty million coulda make all o' dem happy
And this the third rider was mounted on a black stallion
So remember to vote out these horsemen next election

Ah see a horse laughing kee, kee, kee
He say in this country he have more weight than me
60 He say, if you ride a cockhorse to Banbury cross
You stupid! You riding the horse though you can't see the horse
is you boss.

V
Woe unto you! Oh leaders of my land
For aiding and abetting the sin of covetousness in this island
65 And for lending out my money to build facilities for horse
When you breaking down my humble shack with your regiment
and Police Force
But behold! What the prophecy say!
That this the fourth horse e was a mangy grey
70 And the rider on this horse was like unto no man
Because the jockey on this horse was a skellington
So all you be careful all you don't end up like that unfortunate
jockey
Because the Racing Complex is the Lapeyrouse Cemetery

75 Then a headless horse* was laughing at the Racing Authority
Claiming whu happen in Venezuela was a show of solidarity

He say from Creation the horse regard man as he master
That is why he di' run down last for spite at La Rinconda

DELAMO (Franz Lambkin)
Trinidad and Tobago

* *A headless horse* – 'Beheaded' – refers to a successful Trinidad horse of
the late seventies, who performed badly in a Venezuela meet.

Capitalism Gone Mad

You got to be a millionaire
Or some kinda petty bourgeoisie
Anytime you living here
In this country
5 You gotta to be in skullduggery
Making you money illicitly
To live like somebody
In this country
10 It's outrageous and insane
Dem crazy prices in Port of Spain
And like the merchants going out they brain
And the working man, like he only toiling in vain

Where you ever hear?
15 A television
Cost seven thousand
Quarter million for lil piece 'o land
A pair o' sneakers
Two hundred dollars
20 Eighty, ninety thousand for motor cars

At last here in Trinidad
We see: Capitalism gone mad
It sad and getting more bad
Because doux doux Capitalism gone mad.

25 To provide for you family
Today on your present salary
Is an impossibility
In this country
So many bills to pay
30 There's no conceivable way
To save for a rainy day
In this country

Avariciousness to be precise
is why every damn thing so overpriced
35 Big business making everybody feel . . . .
Government gi'e them an open license to steal

Could you believe that
One nylon pantie
Is nineteen ninety
40 Twenty dollars for some baby milk
The cheapest jersey
Cost over sixty
Two hundred and change a yard for silk
It hard here in Trinidad
45 (Lord have mercy) Capitalism gone mad
It sad, things getting more bad
Oh Lord' Capitalism gone bad.

To buy a pack o cigarette
Does leave you with a hole in your wallet
50 And money is so bad to get
In this country
Necessity or luxuries
It doesn't matter what the matter is
They charging anything they please
55 In this country
Primary school books : price is lewd
Is highway robbery the price of food
All hopes and dreams elude the poor man
But politicians still expect good work attitudes

60 Just imagine this:
The cheapest coffin
Over three thousand
Not even dying today easy
Thousands of dollars
65 for the undertakers
So you could get a spot in the cemetery
It hard here in Trinidad
Oh Lord! Capitalism gone mad
The gladness that once we had
70 Is gone because : Capitalism gone mad.

You got to have heavy contacts
Know how to move up in society
To make any kind o' impact
In this country

75 You got to know how to gyp the field
How to scheme and swindle properly
Perfect the art of wheel & deal
In this country
I say survival in this land
80 Isn't easy for no man
With unemployment and high inflation
Some o we go dead before the end of this recession

Whe' the hell is this?
A mango Julie
85 Costing three fifty
Forty dollars for one watermelon
Half you salary
Pork fish meat and poultry
Time yo buy greens: all you money done

90 It hard here in Trinidad
(Lord have mercy!) Capitalism gone mad
It's sad and getting more hard
(Put a hand Lord!) Capitalism gone mad.

SPARROW (Slinger Francisco)
Grenada

Isms/Schisms

I
Grenada, Grenada, the Black Man thank you
Grenadians teach meh mih biggest lesson
And who ain't learn from them I am sorry.
But listen to the lessons Grenadian teach me
They teach me : Capital – Social – or Communism
Is the same gun head all 'o dem on
And from the time you team up with them
Like Grenada you straight on the losing end

My friend, my friend,
Got to stay 'way from them isms
Cause dem ism is confusion
You must have a nuclear weapon
Just to hold on to your ism
One ism with a gun telling you to vote
One say 'Don't Vote' with a gun at your throat

They saving all their arms and ammo for me
And sending their wheat for their enemy,
Got to stay 'way from their isms
For them isms is just schisms

II
From the first time you team with one o' dem isms
The first thing they talking 'bout is protection
Double-tax your people, full your treasury
You got to maintain an efficient army
And too much pressure from the opposition
They could always rent you a whole battalion
And when you get the next ism out the way
How much life it cost you could never say

        No way, no way!
Got to stay way from them isms
For them ism is confusion
You must have a nuclear weapon
Just to hold on to your ism
Rescue mission to help Grenadians
Rescue mission to Afghanistan
Rescue mission going the world over
But no rescue mission to South Africa
Got to stay 'way from them ism
For them ism is just schism

III
Remember when Grenada had 'a ism
That everybody say was Mongoose oppression
The other ism just take up some gun
And they had the whole Mongoose pack on the run
Four years later the ting turn back round
Is the same Mongoose justice preaching in town
And Grenadians keep suffering evermore
All their taxpayers' money going for war
      And more war, and more war
Got to stay way from them ism
Cause them ism is confusion
You must have a nuclear weapon
Just to hold on to your ism
They say how to keep sport from politics
Every four years they boycotting Olympics
And while we arguing about who good and who bad
Them gone out in space and exchanging flag
Got to stay way from them ism
For them ism is just schism.

IV
The time is ripe right now more than ever
For man to sit down and write the new order
Where man would respect a man as a man
And not through colour and superior weapon
When we must be equal, righteous and fair
And realise that the earth is for all to share
And to his fellowman always be true
But until that day come, hear what I goh do

      And you too, and you too
Got to stay way from them ism
Cause them isms is confusion
You must have a nuclear weapon
Just to hold on to your ism
One ism say, 'Come' one ism say, 'Go';
One ism say, 'Yes!' the next one say, 'No!'
And while we keep fighting their 'ism' war
We people keep getting poor and more poor
Got to stay way from them ism
For them ism is just schism.

                  STALIN (Leroy Calliste)
                        Trinidad and Tobago
Note: A different person from the author of 'South Trumpeter'

Sea Water and Sand

I
Man every Caribbean leader
Taking lag at one another
Every one trying to protect his dollar
Especially since Guyana
5 Ain't have no foreign exchange, sah
And with Jamaica devalue she dollar
Well countries who are more wealthy
Man they laughing out kee, kee, kee
And making fun at Guyanese and Jamaican money
10 They can't see in the Caribbean
Unless there is cooperation
All o' them on the same road to destruction.

Is time the Barbadians them understand
You can't sit back and laugh at Jamaicans

15 'Cause without them tourist boats from Reagan
Sweet Barbados heading for starvation
The day you ain't get aid from Washington
Well, crapaud smoke yuh pipe Mr St John
It's time that you and Eugenia Charles understand
20 That all you have is just sea water and sand.

II
All of them Caribbean leader
Instead of pulling together
They prefer to friend with Reagan and Thatcher
Dominicans suffering bad
25 Their goods can't get to Trinidad
'Cause Chambers ain't giving licences; which is sad.
Chambers say he ain't in this big racket
They want to flood Trinidad market
With all their cheap inferior goods, and he won't permit it.
30 But he want BWEE register
As the national carrier
No way sah! Antigua turn down his offer

It's time Chambers and Vere Bird understand
You both need each other in the region
35 You can't make treaties with France and Japan
And with your own people you can't join hands
Mr Bird, them tourists that come St John ('s)
They need BWEE for their transportation
It's time you and Chambers sit down and start to plan
40 'Cause all you have is just sea water and sand

III
Caricom leaders does show zest
The feel that their country is blest
Once they have more foreign exchange than the rest
Others riding high and mighty
45 Claiming they have stability
Cause their dollar in US is worth plenty
And they meeting regularly
Drawing up all kind o' treaty
And after they drink their whisky the treaty dead already
50 At their Heads of Government Conference
Is much shop talk and ignorance
Lots of talk, but no action ever commence.

Is time we Trinidadians understand
We have to help the other small islands
55 We can't eat pitch and oil with rice and jam

We got to trade it for Grenadian yam
All the oil we have in our nation
Is just a drop in the Arabian ocean
And stop telling Guyanese they from the mud land
60 'Cause all we have is just sea water and sand

IV
Some of them Caribbean leader
To get Mr Reagan's dollar
Will denounce their Caricom friends and neighbour
Eugenia cussing Guyana
65 Refusing to even go there
And lambasting Chambers for his behaviour
Chambers vetting Grenadians hey
Man as though they cocobey
Cause to travel to Port of Spain Grenadines need visa
70 LDC's want Trini money
To build up their economy
Still you can't spend a TT dollar in their country

Is time the whole Caribbean understand
We don't have gold, uranium or diamonds,
75 So Yankees don't care if we fall or stand
Our resources can't change Reagan's war plan
You can't depend on tourists, John Compton
To carry St Lucians into heaven
To survive, you and Simmonds must walk hand in hand
80 Cause nobody can't eat sea water and sand

MIGHTY CHALKDUST (Hollis Liverpool)
Trinidad and Tobago

Carnival Rhapsody

Beat dem drums
Boys beat dem drums,
Fast and loud and sweet,
Dey go ge we consolation,
5 Dey go ease we sufferation,
Down Frederick Street,
Down Frederick Street,

So beat dem drums
Boys beat dem drums,
10 'Til Federation come
Den we go jump in time
To the Creole rhyme,
Around de town.
Around de town.

15 And beat dem drums
Boys beat dem drums,
'Til de Jour-Vert Monday comes
When de Judge jump up,
In de parson's frock,
20 And de Doctor play de clown.

So beat dem drums
Boys beat dem drums,
Look! ah feel de rhythm in me spine,
Ah feel de rhythm,
25 In me chac-chac wine,
Shaking me far behind.

And beat dem drums
Boys beat dem drums,
Ah feel de rhythm in me soul,
30 Ah feel de rhythm in me Creole blood,
E go stap wid me 'til ah ole.
E go stap wid me 'til ah ole.

KNOLLY LA FORTUNE
Trinidad and Tobago

Pan Run II

Ah make 10 years
10 years and 12 strokes
ah mih eyes send
de water stretching
5 dong mih face
wid every lash
scarring mih flesh
like mih pan
ah leff carve out
10 on de jail wall
So ah crossing over now
ah say ah crossing over now
clear de way
leh mih pass
15 please mih ass
dis is war.

To hell an back
to hell
behind de bridge
20 an all ah we blood
crawling cross de City
like de dry river
an ah keep seeing
de La Basse picture
25 Kobo black like we
an shitting dong
– white –
an from de dark
stinking manhole
30 ah screaming
10 years an 12 strokes
10 years an 12 strokes
all over town
an dem people in House
35 fraid mih voice
an dem others up
in Balcony too far
from mih mudder belly
to see mih tossing
40 in de night.

So before de sun
did rise one day
ah get Baptize
an mih Mudder
45 children was right dey
singing hymns
to light mih way
an when ah went
on de moaning ground
50 ah start to travel
ah start to see
Blood like fire
running cross de sea
an all mih Mudder
55 children bawling
an drowning in
dey own blood
an ah start to bawl
wid dem
60 10 YEARS AN 12 STROKES
10 YEARS AN 12 STROKES
over and over
in God ears
Yes in God ears
65 till ah rise up from Africa
in de spirit
washed in de blood
of de Lamb
buh no other fount
70 I know buh de wappie
table an de Cassa
saving mih when ah lorse
an mih blood flowing
mad when ah broken
75 like de dry river
coming dong
coming dong
cross de City
an looking vex
80 to kill.

Fisheye – Batasby –
Jules – Ellie – Spree –
Sarge – Bully – Mastifae –
all yuh know
85 how mih blood

did come in de yard
all yuh smell
mih woman sweat
after we did breed
90 de fire under
she belly
an now ah longing
fuh she ah longing
fuh she
95 sweet tones
ah see she
ah hear she
buh she leff mih hand
hard and trembling
100 J'Ouvert morning.

Negro-gram did play mas
in de rumshop
by de market
in de square
105 an all bout
TRINIDAD
de whe-whe man
buss de mark
an dem Police an all
110 did play – BALISIER –
an de shango man
beat de Babu man
out ah town
whu de smart man say?
115 whu de doctor say?
Crier man is 10 years
an 12 strokes
whu de Doc did say?
MASSA DAY DONE!
120 an de kaiso man did
raise he voice too
from de cage
fuh all dem saga boys
Jean & Dinah
125 de Yankees gorn!
So crash dem
programme dong doctor
an dem Baptist
could stand up
130 an rock back

an shout now
like me
puh dong mih name
on de roll
135 I'za runner
on dis fucking
project

Who is me?
look ole man
140 an come fuh
mih woman
Who is me?
I is she master
I is master
145 of Iron an
it in mih blood!
Who is me?
I is de blood
yuh raising
150 fuh 10 years
an woman
you is mih child mudder
an I is mih Mudder
chile in nature
155 Since When?
Since from de Iron
cradle of Benin and Ife!
Yoruba thunder travel far
in wood an tight skin
160 like lightening in de storm
WE IN – SINCE THEN – an
blast out sound from metal
in mih blood
in mih chile – now –
165 like ah piano

So come!
leh we play togedda!
Gimmih it quick! O Gord
lemmih hear de notes so high
170 Lemmih hear de Iron scream
Hot! hot! fuh all dem strokes,
now lissen to mih voice
calling deep – deep from
de dust pain drum

175 . . .an mih blood
     never stop running
     cross mih middle passage. . .

DELANO ABDUL MALIK DECOTEAU
                        Grenada

Kaisoman

     ah come from far,
     very far,
     see de scar?
     i eh no third world man
 5   i eh no second world man
     i is first world man
     i am two point four million old
     years and more

     in mih darkness
10   is me. . . . I who first see
     de light
     and ah used to play drums
     ah de best
     getting rhythm and movement
15   and feeling
     pounding mih talented fists
     on mih chest
     in dem days it din have
     no vest

20   an i use to be a praise singer
     going morning to night
     composing and memorising
     from village to village
     entertaining community, chief
25   and king

     i. . . . . .me, an early poet
     man wise wid words
     dropping words for wise men
     to sift
30   until dey get de drift

     *(Calypso chant and
     drumming begin)*

is me. . . . . .me
kaisoman
man talking to men
brought in chains to dis land
35 to be chantelle, bois man, stickman
petit quart in mih han'
serenading and masqueraders
shouting:
Kaiso! Kaiso! singgg kaisoman
40 rhyme! rhyme!
sing and whine

c'est l'avantage, belle bois garcon
an ah bravadajj

sing away kaisoman sing
45 sing Kaiser Willyam
Britain win de war
sing! not even for ah token
sing! drink grog, but stay broken
louder! we wanta hear
50 louder! kaisoman sing

but sing smutty sing stink
here take ah nex' drink
Britain win de war!
more kaisoman more
55 sing and doh think
sing humour sing leggo
sing hardship sing death blows
sing bout priest sing bout nun
yuh is attilla de hun
60 de roaring lion
yuh is growling tiger, dictator,
gibraltar, unknown, executor
all roll in one

is me. . . . . .me, kaisoman
65 go! go! bring bamboo
it getting close to lent
forget chairs, get tarpaulin,
open Kaiso tent we eh have ah cent
i is ah diehard social commentator
70 ah born agitator and ah wicked philosopher
i is ah bard and ah bad

like sparrow 'jean and dinah'
i is kitchener 'jerico and 'de vengeance
ah moko'

75 oh! what a country
oh! what an awful place
man dis country so nice
dat valentino's dogs stop barking
dey encircling, dey attacking, dey biting

80 is me. . . . . .me Kaisoman
frightened, stifled, trifled
pushed in ah corner – bridled
sung no praises! given no honour!
for no solid reason
85 ah like mango vert
all dey gih mih is just one season
as if dey expec' mih to eat rhyme
and swallow reason!

man is bedlam man is boredom
90 is murder, is mayhem
before me, classics, pop songs
even billy graham
wid mih fifty-fifty vision
ah better than television
95 wid mih critical voice
ah surpass radio station

cut mih throat
because i am ah good surgeon
examine me
100 because ah like to examine
de sick belly of dis nation
while ah rhyming, ah riddling
operating in de oral tradition

is me kaisoman . . . . . harmonising lyrics
105 is me kaisoman . . . . . sermonising politics
is me kaisoman . . . . . me and mih controversial
topics
is me. . . . . .me. . . . . .meeeeeeee kaisoman
TELLING IT LIKE IT IS.

LASANA KWESI
Guyana

A Voice from de Grave

Long time now I buildin
an' buildin dis foundation
of meh soul.
My house was ah house ah dreams
5 My house was ah house ah schemes
My house ent finish yet.
I did get de contract long time now
to shape de tenor of meh voice,
to build ah home of meh choice.
10 Ah put meh han' down in ah bin,
fine ah tin, take ah hint
cause deep inside de steel
ah dis soul ah mine
ah follow ah beat in meh head
15   till ah dead

Ah groove dese notes deep deep
long time now when drum
was cheap.
Was heaps ah rubbish
20 in de street.
from bamboo to Tamboo
from pillar to post
ah beat meh body,
fine meh voice, plenty noise,
25 etch meh name in search fuh fame,
all direction, every section of dis
        nation

Long time now I buildin dis house
meh house ent finish yet
30 Ah did play wid fire once yuh
        know,
While some ah dem was bendin'
        wire
I din res till ah could express
35 dis soun' an' take dis town by
storm down town.
Ah did play wid fire once
till ah taste de heat o' de cat
on meh back like de sun
40 dat bun de tenor of meh dreams
Ah did play wid fire once
Was de heat ah hell ah did face

dem days
From La Cou Harpe to John John,
45 from Laventille to Hell Yard ah
    bad bad bad like crab
ah did roam like de devil in hell
till meh voice spread roun town
down town
50 all roun'
Long time now I buildin dis house
meh house ent finish yet.

I wage meh war eh, like Jab
  Malasie geh meh money,
55 cut meh way, blade to blade,
    bolt to bolt, blood fuh blood.
From yard to yard ah gone mad mad
wid invention
Meh tune reach heaven wid good
60 intention
An Papa God did smile when I
    play
dat fus note. He smile. While
De saints dem dance when deh
65   hear
de cord in meh throat
Poopa dat was fete! Dat was fete!

Ever since dat day ah gay fu so.
Is Spree fuh so. Dat is me.
70 ah drinkin' rum, ah beating drum
ah watch dem fellas take ah note.
From Ellie to Jules
from Tony to Bertie
from Bar Twenty to Red Army
75 from Fascinators to Invaders
I follow de rhythm fuh years in
    meh soul

Long time now I buildin' dis house
My house was ah house ah dreams
80 my house ent finish yet.

Is blight I blight we. Is blight
  I blight.
Lord jus so, jus so
de bass ah meh life stop beatin'.

85 de stroke in meh leg start
   throbin'
to de hour when dem pan start
   playin'
from Church to de cemetry

90 from Church to de cemetry
deh carry me to bury me
without ah shelter on meh back

and dem tenor did ring out loud
de crowd keep swellin out
95 like one thousand bass drum
   beatin', beatin'
from Church to de cemetry

from grave to grave brave brave
ah face de heat
100 without ah shelter on meh back
without ah shelter on meh back

an pan have canopy. yes, pan
have canopy.

from Church to de cemetry
105 deh sponsor me in song
all dem days ah live in town

an' meh house ent finish yet
Lord! meh house ent finish yet.

something wrong.
110 something wrong.

JOSEPH CUMMINGS
Trinidad and Tobago

The house in this poem is symbolic. The pan-man in our society is both poet and artist rolled into one. Against a background of hardship and depravity he has struggled and is still struggling to build his home. To me, this dream, this constant longing for a complete and durable recognition is as elusive as the home that Spree never saw. Spree's experience then, as I see it, is representative of a hope and a promise still unfulfilled. And so one can hear Spree's voice raising from the grave in protest as he cries.
                                             J. Cummings

Pan Drama

Ex-
it
mas' man
push on
5 pan man,
a man
attuned, trapped

caught (like me)
making
10 subtle inden-
tations
in his
spider web

(now)
15 limbo-
ing from flambeau –
pan-yard
to
flying Pan Am

20 a-
massing cultural
missions

(then)
bombing down
25 the town
down

Frederick Street

to chipping feet
featly Jouvert
30 morning.

Wheeling across
the whole
cultural pan-
orama

35 now (like you)
armed only

with my
rubber ended sticks

sick of your
40 blurred bourgeois
smile

pinging
              and
                          ponging
45 calypso tunes
of
chamber pot drama

or
racial melodrama

50 for colourless
mocking folk from
far away smog
lands
who

55 smiling
or
like the dull
eyed miss
mincing
60 dutch
sausage sandwiches
sighing

'mom they steal
the show

65 for
how attuned
they are
to their
base tenor
70 of living'.

Trapped
attuned

making subtle
indentations
75 in my
spider web

I wheel away.

VICTOR QUESTEL
Trinidad and Tobago

Calypso Dancers

You should have seen them
dancing the Calypso –
the whirling
strutting
5 sidling
shuffling
jumping
twisting
tripping
10 turning
leaping
crossing
capering
crashing Calypso!
15 Now with a whirl and a toss and turn
and a tumbling;
Calypso!
Now with a slipping and a shouting and a sliding,
Ecstasy!
20 And then with a mock-slow
sinuous winding,
tortuous rhythm translated into body.

To see them is to see the wind
as ocean sees it,
25 frenzied.
To touch them
is to touch the ocean
horizon-like, ever and never.
To join them is to let the senses perish
30 or swelter in a hot coagulation
of joy and drunken stupor,
to lose all consciousness of having self or sinew –

headless,
armless,
35 legless,
bosomless, – breathless –
retaining only
a vague, yet wildly burning
Sense of Rhythm.

40 *Music is fire,*
and rhythm is the smoke
that leaps from it,
wetting the eyes,
drugging the veins,
45 *threading a delicate poison*
in, through, between the rapid folds
of mind, like – in a grey noon –
beyond the mist, round a mass of brain-cloud –
coiled –
50 *a skein of lightning, – but hotter –*
a web of warm pulsation.
Sensuous Calypso!

Look at their faces,
each a sweating mask,
55 a frozen crescendo of passion.
Look at their eyes, –
Can you read your way into a teardrop? –
Heaven!
There are mirrors of emotion fretting the quivering lids. . .
60 A smile snakes its way
round and round
their mouths,
loading the flesh with ripples,
ripples, ripples,
65 ripples everywhere; from the greasy chasms
on their foreheads
to the hairy palisades
drawn up about their eyes, protecting
prism beyond prism,
70 each gushing a spectrum of radiating madness.

Music is a demon,
and rhythm is the spell
that sits upon his eye
and looks
75 *a happy frenzy into mortal bones. . .*

160

Maddening Calypso!

Look at their hands –
shoving
twisting
80 striking
clutching hands.
Look at their bodies,
lurching closer . . . closer . . .
then dissolving, each –
85 spiral after spiral –
into each; and then
resolving themselves into a twain
convulsive –
lurching farther . . . farther . . .

90 These are not men and women, entities
divorced, diverse, or free.
These are one rolling
rollicking
weaving, winding,
95 sweating, shouting
expression
of a passion universal,
urged, quickened and controlled
by an insistent blast
100 of wild resistless rhythm.

Music has form and colour,
Rhythm has force –
Music is a river,
men are the strengthless stones
105 *swept on and on. . .*
Music is a wave,
men are the bubbly foam
rising and falling through infinitudes of cadence.
Music is a call, men are the echo.
110 *Music is a whip,*
and men are slaves
groaning in a spasm of vibrant toil.
Dynamic Calypso!

They cannot stop,
115 These dancers, until it stops,
until it has expressed the final drop of awakened passion. . .
Men say the earth is a vital graveyard

161

of its own history,
that every fold of rock
120 teems
with imprisoned residues of an exhausted age.
So is music –
so is the music of the Calypso –
centuries of warm compulsion
125 spinning a woof of fire –
screaming, wriggling, whirling, flexing fire –
around the hot commotion
of dancing feet;
welling up
130 in crazy crescendos
through crevices of maddening sound, –
pulsating aeons instantly unwombed,
charred passions, fossil emotions
cast up in
135 rhythmic spurts of undulating dance. . .

It will not stop,
They *cannot* stop.
Forever
you shall see them dancing
140 The Calypso.

ELSWORTH KEANE
St Vincent

The Mighty Intriguer

Last month was me last pay day,
I ain't going see no more pay,
Me shirt is just rip and fray,
I hungry the livelong day,
5 A dollar won't even stray
Across old Intriguer way.
                              What wrong?
The boss tell me wend me way,
The boss tell me wend me way.

10 But me Carnival money
        Salted away.
I bank for the fancy
        Mas' I going play.

Ballade going tickle
15   The high and the low;
Intriguer going make it
        New in calypso.

Small farmers, they making moan,
They wasting their sweat and brawn.
20 Cassava won't grow 'pon stone,
Drought suck the land dry as bone.
Alice touch me for a loan,
Intriguer lie back and groan,
                        And she?
25 Pick up petticoat and gone,
Pick up petticoat and gone.

Don't ask me from where I
        Going get me next pay;
But me Carnival coppers
30   Salted away,
Ballade going tickle
        The high and the low;
Intriguer going make it
Brand new in calypso.

                        SLADE HOPKINSON
                        Guyana

The Spoiler's Return
For Earl Lovelace

I sit high on this bridge in Laventille,
watching that city where I left no will
but my own conscience and rum-eaten wit,
and limers passing see me where I sit,
5 ghost in brown gabardine, bones in a sack,
and bawl: 'Ay, Spoiler, boy! When you come back?'
And those who bold don't feel they out of place
to peel my limeskin back, and see a face
with eyes as cold as a dead macajuel,
10 and if they still can talk, I answer: 'Hell.'
I have a room there where I keep a crown,
and Satan send me to check out this town.
Down there, that Hot Boy have a stereo
where, whole day, he does blast my caiso;

                                        163

15 I beg him two weeks' leave and he send me
    back up, not as no bedbug or no flea,
    but in this limeskin hat and floccy suit,
    to sing what I did always sing: the truth.
    Tell Desperadoes when you reach the hill,
20 I decompose, but I composing still:

    I going to bite them young ladies, partner,
    like a hot dog or a hamburger
    and if you thin, don't be in a fright
    is only big fat women I going to bite.

25 The shark, racing the shadow of the shark
    across clear coral rocks, does makes them dark –
    that is my premonition of the scene
    of what passing over this Caribbean.
    Is crab climbing crab-back, in a crab-quarrel,
30 and going round and round in the same barrel,
    is sharks with shirt-jacs, sharks with well-pressed fins,
    ripping we small fry off with razor grins;
    nothing ain't change but colour and attire,
    so back me up, Old Brigade of Satire,
35 back me up, Martial, Juvenal, and Pope
    (to hang theirself I giving plenty rope),
    join Spoiler' chorus, sing the song with me,
    Lord Rochester, who praised the nimble flea:

    Were I, who to my cost already am
40 *One of those strange, prodigious creatures, Man,*
    A spirit free, to choose from my own share,
    What case of flesh and blood I pleased to wear,
    I hope when I die, after burial,
    To come back as an insect or animal.

45 I see these islands and I feel to bawl,
    'area of darkness' with VS Nightfall.

    Lock off your tears, you casting pearls of grief
    on a duck's back, a waxen dasheen leaf,
    the slime crab's carapace is waterproof
50 and those with hearing aids turn off the truth,
    and their dark glasses let you criticize
    your own presumptuous image in their eyes.
    Behind dark glasses is just hollow skull,
    and black still poor, though black is beautiful.
55 So, crown and mitre me Bedbug the First –

the gift of mockery with which I'm cursed
is just a insect biting Fame behind,
a vermin swimming in a glass of wine,
that, dipped out with a finger, bound to bite
60 its saving host, ungrateful parasite,
whose sting, between the cleft arse and its seat,
reminds Authority man is just meat,
a moralist as mordant as the louse
that the good husband brings from the whorehouse,
65 the flea whose itch to make all Power wince,
will crash a fete, even at his life's expense,
and these pile up in lime pits by the heap,
daily, that our deliverers may sleep.
All those who promise free and just debate,
70 then blow up radicals to save the state,
who allow, in democracy's defense,
a parliament of spiked heads on a fence,
all you go bawl out, 'Spoils, things ain't so bad.'
This ain't the Dark Age, is just Trinidad,
75 is human nature, Spoiler, after all,
it ain't big genocide, is just bohbohl;
safe and conservative, 'fraid to take side,
they say that Rodney commit suicide,
is the same voices that, in the slave ship,
80 smile at their brothers, 'Boy, is just the whip,'
I free and easy, you see me have chain?
A little censorship can't cause no pain,
a little graft can't rot the human mind,
what sweet in goat-mouth sour in his behind.
85 So I sing with Attila, I sing with Commander,
what right in Guyana, right in Uganda.
The time could come, it can't be very long,
when they will jail calypso for picong,
for first comes television, then the press,
90 all in the name of Civic Righteousness;
it has been done before, all Power has
made the sky shit and maggots of the stars,
over these Romans lying on their backs,
the hookers swaying their enormous sacks,
95 until all language stinks, and the truth lies,
a mass for maggots and a fete for flies;
and, for a spineless thing, rumor can twist
into a style the local journalist –
as bland as a green coconut, his manner
100 routinely tart, his sources the Savannah
and all pretensions to a native art

reduced to giggles at the coconut cart,
where heads with reputations, in one slice,
are brought to earth, when they ain't eating nice;
105 and as for local Art, so it does go,
the audience have more talent than the show.

Is Carnival, straight Carnival that's all,
the beat is base, the melody bohbohl,
all Port of Spain is a twelve-thirty show,
110 some playing Kojak, some Fidel Castro,
some Rastamen, but, with or without locks,
to Spoiler is the same old khaki socks,
all Frederick Street stinking like a closed drain,
Hell is a city much like Port of Spain,
115 what the rain rots, the sun ripens some more,
all in due process and within the law,
as, like a sailor on a spending spree,
we blow our oil-bloated economy
on projects from here to eternity,
120 and Lord, the sunlit streets break Spoiler's heart,
to have natural gas and not to give a fart,
to see them line up, pitch-oil tin in hand:
each independent, oil-forsaken island,
like jeering at some scrunter with the blues,
125 while you lend him some need-a-half-sole shoes,
some begging bold as brass, some coming meeker,
but from Jamaica to poor Dominica
we make them know they begging, every loan
we send them is like blood squeezed out of stone,
130 and giving gives us back the right to laugh
that we couldn't see we own black people starve,
and, more we give, more we congratulate
we-self on our own self-sufficient state.
In all them project, all them Five-Year Plan,
135 what happen to the Brotherhood of Man?
Around the time I dead it wasn't so,
we sang the Commonwealth of caiso,
we was in chains, but chains made us unite,
now who have, good for them, and who blight, blight;
140 my bread is bitterness, my wine is gall,
my chorus is the same: 'I want to fall.'
Oh, wheel of industry, check out your cogs!
Between the knee-high trash and khaki dogs
Arnold's phoenician trader reach this far,
145 selling you half-dead batteries for your car;
the children of Tagore, in funeral shroud,

curry favor and chicken from the crowd;
as for the Creoles, check their house, and look,
you bust your brain before you find a book,
150 when Spoiler see all this, ain't he must bawl,
'area of darkness,' with VS Nightfall?
Corbeaux like cardinals line the La Basse
in ecumenical patience while you pass
the Beetham Highway – Guard corruption's stench,
155 you bald, black justices of the High Bench –
and beyond them the firelit mangrove swamps,
ibises practicing for postage stamps,
Lord, let me take a taxi South again
and hear, drumming across Caroni Plain,
160 the tabla in the Indian half hour
when twilight fills the mud huts of the poor,
to hear the tattered flags of drying corn
rattle a sky from which all the gods gone,
their bleached flags of distress waving to me
165 from shacks, adrift like rafts on a green sea,
'Things ain't go change, they ain't go change at all,'
to my old chorus: 'Lord, I want to bawl.'
The poor still poor, whatever arse they catch.
Look south from Laventille, and you can watch
170 the torn brown patches of the Central Plain
slowly restitched by needles of the rain,
and the frayed earth, crisscrossed like bagasse,
spring to a cushiony quilt of emerald grass,
and who does sew and sow and patch the land?
175 The Indian. And whose villages turn sand?
The fishermen doomed to stitching the huge net
of the torn foam from Point to La Fillette.

One thing with Hell, at least it organize
in soaring circles, when any man dies
180 he must pass through them first, that is the style,
Jesus was down here for a little while,
cadaverous Dante, big-guts Rabelais,
all of them wave to Spoiler on their way.
Catch us in Satan tent, next carnival:
185 Lord Rochester, Quevedo, Juvenal,
Maestro, Martial, Pope, Dryden, Swift, Lord Byron,
the lords of irony, the Duke of Iron,
hotly contending for the monarchy
in couplets or the old re-minor key,
190 all those who gave earth's pompous carnival
fatigue, and groaned 'O God, I feel to fall!'

all those whose anger for the poor on earth
made them weep with a laughter beyond mirth,
names wide as oceans when compared with mine
195 salted my songs, and gave me their high sign.
All you excuse me, Spoiler was in town;
you pass him straight, so now he gone back down.

DEREK WALCOTT
St Lucia

Book So Deep

de beat goes on
and de never ending river
of degree hungry people
flushin down
5 rushin down
thru dis valley of mardness
see dem people
course riding
and hiding
10 from reality
in de shadows of success

de beat goes on
and on in UWI
because all ah we
15 get sentence
to four years hard labour
three years good behaviour
in dis concentration camp

and I is just ah prisoner
20 just ah prisoner
in dis penal colony
behind de barb wire
of mental agony

BOOK SO DEEP

25 it left meh in ah daze
tryin to find meh way
outa dis maze

168

takin nite to make day
to stay in dis
30 intellectual rat race

look at meh class mates
meh cell mates
hustlin one anodda
jostlin forever
35 dey brain in cold sweat
just to get
dat BSC
– intellectual property –
at any cost
40 even if dey spit on we

BOOK SO DEEP

ah have to get up
to get down
down in dis mental plantation
45 chain to de strain
of ah imperial brainwash
and de brain slave master
standing dey on page one
wid he gun . . . barking
50 and he whip snarling
in we head

– study an' dead –

mouldin
and rollin we out
55 ah dis mental assembly plant
just in time
to stand de grind
in de production line
wid we unemployed
60 brodder an' sister
lookin fo' wuk

so yuh mean
yuh didn't know
dat UWI
65 is ah brain slave market
wey de local and foreign
big business

could purchase
ah broken graduate
70 cuffed, collared
and tagged
for de free enterprise

de beat goes on
but yuh ain't have time
75 for dancin
man de BOOK SO DEEP
only ah nervous breakdown
could bring yuh down in time

is ah high tension cram
80 to survive
dis crash program exam
dey say
who make make
who break. . .hard luck
85 if yuh brain ain't strong
yuh cyar take it
so head or tail
some go pass
and some go fail
90 some go end up
in de jail
for de writing
on de wall
in ah sweaty 107

95 — can you really make it? —
dat is de question
de six million dollar question

and de bionic book junkies
caught up in de mainstream
100 end up in ah daydream
face to face
wid suicide
face to face
wid policeman gun
105 face to face
wid frustration
and still wouldn't
FACE REALITY

BOOK SO DEEP

110   man jumpin off
de Nat Sci building
to get down
in ah hurry

one gorn
115   plenty more to go
in dis never ending
brain squeeze
and de beat goes on

so even self
120   de riot squad
board de campus
to beat we arse
dey ain't diggin nutten
because BOOK SO DEEP
125   dat de beat
goes orn as usual

BOOK SO DEEP

dat dey life book up
dey attitudes book up

130   BOOK SO DEEP

and still
de mickey mouse
dolly house politicians
tryin to tie we up
135   wid skin tight analysis
and still
dem radical intellectual
clad in workin class clothes
dealing out
140   ruling class blows
on de side –

enjoy yuh ride
professor

ah go bide meh time

145 BOOK SO DEEP

is too much mardness
for one man to take

BOOK TOO DEEP

to get pass out
150 ah bound to hold out
wid all meh heart
and soul
in these dreadful times

so hang on to yuh mind
155 and keep yuh head orn
bound to block up
against
de miseducation
brain squeezer
160 foreign
indoctrinator
brain slave dealer
and tho' de book so deep
no hill too steep
165 for we to climb
in we push
to shake down
dis prison of progress

BROTHER RESISTANCE
Trinidad and Tobago

Man to Pan
(From pages 73–78)

was like a return to me
was spree finding spree
not in chains but free

was all o that and deeper
5 was the dream
returning to the sleeper
was the stream
returning to the river

was the river
10 returning to the sea
was all o that and deeper

it kinda hard to explain
after 400 years of pain
but to tell you de truth
15 i ain't think ah go looking for
any sorta roots
i from trinidad
and ah like it bad
i ain't know wha ah go looking for
20 or wha to expect
i ain't go to resurrect
any ghosts i long time forget
it ain't as if i go hoping for
a welcome home fete
25 like dry mud hugging oletalk rain

de mudderland opening she hand:
'eh eh where you been all dis time boy?
i hear you playing steelband
since you cross de atlantic
30 you is one big man
you forget is i teach you to beat stick
anyhow i forgive you
i know wha four century
could do to you memory'

35 no it wasn't like that
it kinda hard to explain
after 400 years of pain
but even though ah say spree boy just go
do like limbo
40 let your body flow
don't put fancy notion in you brain
yet ah find when ah step off de plane
it kinda hard to explain

was like a return to me
45 was spree finding spree
not in chains but free

was all o that and deeper
was the dream
returning to the sleeper

50 was the stream
returning to the river
was the river
returning to the sea
was all o that and deeper

55 ah say yes well ah tell you pardner
dis is it you reach dis is africa
you go lick down palm wine like rum
you go hear plenty drum
you go hug up earthriddum woman
60 the ah tell meself
you start again?
wipe dem fancy notion from your brain
don't bring you bad
habits from trinidad
65 till to africa
take it cool take it cool
born slow born slow
400 years you been in de womb
by now you should know
70 to born slow
born slow
forget fancy notion
limbo in slow motion
and as ah turn to touch ground
75 with this offering of steel sound
ah feel a funny feeling
as if ah dreaming
as if ah been here before
it never happen to you?
80 as if ah go walk down a street
and bound to meet
up with somebody ah know
manette jules fisheye
one o dem fellas go stop and say
85 'eh eh spree you here too?
like trinidad move out?
wha going on nuh wha going on?
leh we fire one leh we fire one'
ah had was to tell meself
90 spree keep you head on
you is a long long way from john-john
still ah get de feeling again
it kinda hard to explain

was like a return to me
95 was spree finding spree
    not in chains but free

    but even as ah tread de peace
    of mudder ground
    ah couldn't help wonder if it go be hard
100 to find mih way around
    ah mean it ain't like walking through panyard
    was more like walking through the middle
    of another passage
    with four century excess luggage
105 but sudden so in the middle
    i remember the answer to the riddle
    ONE RED ONE BLACK
    ONE LICKING THE OTHER BOTTOM

                                        POT ON FIRE
110   POT ON FIRE
    you wrong
    you wrong
    answer spider
    try again
115 try again
    ONE RED ONE BLACK
    ONE LICKING THE OTHER BOTTOM
    then in the groove of mih brain
    the answer come
120   P–A–N   P–A–N
                    PAN/ON/FIRE
                    PAN/ON/FIRE
                            you hear me spider?
    but spider didn't reply
125 and ah swear to god
    in de circle of me eye
    ah see spider leave he web
    and taking flight to the sky
    ah say jesus wha is dis?
130 you eye playing tricks
    ah say spree boy you must be weary
    is jet lag from the journey
    you better get some sleep

                            like a axe splitting mih brain
135   it kinda hard to explain
    but what ah thought was spider thread
                            was shango climbing

175

on a chain
of sound
with a smile
of lightning

140

and mih foot root to mudder ground
ah didn't have to go no further
ah didn't have to wait for thunder
145 ah know
was a return to me
ja ja romy-o
was spree finding spree
ja ja romy-o
150 not in chains but free
ja ja romy-o
and as ah stand up deh
in that web of light
ah feel like panorama night
155 and ah hear meself say
oyo oyo
oyo shango
ah glad to see you man
accept this offering
160 of pan
is you drum come home
what i borrow
i return
oyo oyo
165 oyo shango
accept this offering
of pan

JOHN AGARD
Guyana

Parang and Hosay

Hawk
For Oliver Jackman

Leaves shudder the drizzle's shine
like a treng-ka-treng from the cuatros,
beads fly from the tension line.
Gabilan, ay, gabilan,
5 high shadow, pitiless!
The old men without teeth,
rum-guzzlers, country fiddlers,
their rum-heads golden lakes
of a fabulous Yucatan,
10 Gabilan, ay, gabilan!

Caribs, like toothless tigers;
talons raking, a flash,
arrows like twanging wires,
catgut and ocelot,
15 merciless, that is man,
Gabilan, eh, gabilan?
Arima to Sangre Grande,
your wings like extended hands,
a grandee waltzing alone,
20 alone, to the old parang.

Gabilan, ay, gabilan,
the negroes, bastards, mestizos,
proud of their Spanish blood,
of the flesh, dripping like wires,
25 praising your hook, gabilan.
Above their slack mouths the hawk
floats tautly out of the cedars,
leaves the limbs shaking.

Slaves yearn for their master's talons,
30 the spur and the cold, gold eyes,
for the whips, whistling like wires,

time for our turn, gabilan!
But this hawk above Rampanalgas
rasps the sea with raw cries.
35 Hawks have no music.

DEREK WALCOTT
St Lucia

Hosay

I
See me talking,
see me talking,
I beating the drum,
I beating the drum.
5 See me talking,
see me swaying,
left foot right foot
left foot cross,
left foot right foot
10 left foot cross.

See me beating,
I beating the dhole,
left hand on leather
and stick in the right.
15 Swing the waist,
sidestep slap,
swing the arms,
bang the belly.

Look mi brothers
20 tickling the tassas,
drumming their heat,
rolling and rapping,
tapping and cracking,
until they cool
25 and lie limp.

ghang
Hear the cymbal
ghang
crash and roll,
30 ghang ghang

lash and ring,
ghang
ring and lash.

and step on the left
35 and swing on the hip,
swinging the mother
and I slap her belly
and pound her behind.

cross foot
40 swing

II
crab-back belly
inch in a line
furrowing the street,
laying seeds of sound
45 in the echos of heartbeats
throbbing roots under the
rattle of gravel
bearing the flags
like the arrows of canes
50 reaped in a battle
and drown cannes-brulees.

Burn the straw,
heat she up
to fire our hearts
55 and roll many tongues
of women praying
for the dead,
the living in battle.

Inch forward again
60 and bang the world
and quick the meteors
of living skin and clay
until they cool and
buried in fire
65 rise again

Burn till the skull pop.
We rise again.
Brothers in arms

beat their chests,
70 pound the ground,
advance and bring
the flags.

III
Innocent homage
to fighters for freedom,
75 killers of tyrants,
glitter and sparkle
in the campfires of
drums.
Ride on the throb
80 of seas of deep
sound;
ships sent burning
on a wishing wind.

Tombs of children
85 gather in clouds,
haunt the warriors,
spur on the drums
to thunder in the womb
to the scudding patter
90 of small feet echoing
in the halls of our
fathers' tombs.
Small deaths
of uncertain futures
95 ending in a bang
and a bang
and a bang.

IV
Now come the big night.
Boom Ching-a-ching Ching
100 Boom Ching-a-ching Boom
Ching-a-ching Boom.
Towering tadjahs born in a crowd,
shadowed by straw
burning the backsides
105 of drums
of drums
of drums.

Licks on the drums
serve under our hands
110 carve the crowd,
yes,
carve the crowd
with axes
of sound.
115 Rock forward booming
bow sprit,
crash the surf
on a people's troubled
reef,
120 rattle the spray,
wash the spirit
home
home
home.

125 Dance the frenzy the fire
battle clash dance,
leap and circle,
crash the bois,
beat the skull of my world
130 till I cool and lie limp.

Dance the frenzy the fire
the moon,
dance the lunatic,
whirl and orbit
135 the skull of my world
till I am dizzy
and have to change the bearer.

Dance again
and flash the crescent,
140 sickling to reap
the stars,
the glittering tombs
castles in heaven.

V
Dare the daytime
145 with a dancing moon,
parade before the sun,
mimic its heat with burning straw,

show the flame's shadow
bent against the road
150 and drive the drum
in that burning crotch
so that it cries out
and calls the world
to answer.

VI
155 Calls the world
to remember
when
later
the tadjahs take
160 land's farewell
for the horizon's cold wedge.

Bubbles of phosphor dance free
the rippling tombs
refracted in starlight,
165 sinking to meet the mirrored moon,
swirling away to another life.

VII
I am silent now
as I caress the moaning skin
of a grounded drum
170 and trace that
tear's dusty path.

I am silent now.
I done talk.
Until a mounting fire
175 stretches me taut
to move the air again.

CHRISTOPHER LAIRD
Trinidad and Tobago

Monologues

The Saddhu of Couva
For Kenneth Ramchand

When sunset, a brass gong,
vibrate through Couva,
is then I see my soul, swiftly unsheathed,
like a white cattle bird growing more small
5 over the ocean of the evening canes,
and I sit quiet, waiting for it to return
like a hog-cattle blistered with mud,
because, for my spirit, India is too far.
And to that gong
10 sometimes bald clouds in saffron robes assemble
sacred to the evening,
sacred even to Ramlochan,
singing Indian hits from his jute hammock
while evening strokes the flanks
15 and silver horns of his maroon taxi,
as the mosquitoes whine their evening mantras,
my friend Anopheles, on the sitar,
and the fireflies making every dusk Divali.

I knot my head with a cloud,
20 my white mustache bristle like horns,
my hands are brittle as the pages of Ramayana.
Once the sacred monkeys multiplied like branches
in the ancient temples; I did not miss them,
because these fields sang of Bengal,
25 behind Ramlochan Repairs there was Uttar Pradesh;
but time roars in my ears like a river,
old age is a conflagration
as fierce as the cane fires of crop time.
I will pass through these people like a cloud,
30 they will see a white bird beating the evening sea
of the canes behind Couva,
and who will point it as my soul unsheathed?
Neither the bridegroom in beads,
nor the bride in her veils,
35 their sacred language on the cinema hoardings.

I talked too damn much on the Couva Village Council.
I talked too softly, I was always drowned
by the loudspeakers in front of the stores
or the loudspeakers with the greatest pictures.
40 I am best suited to stalk like a white cattle bird
on legs like sticks, with sticking to the Path
between the canes on a district road at dusk.
Playing the Elder. There are no more elders.
Is only old people.

45 My friends spit on the government.
I do not think is just the government.
Suppose all the gods too old,
Suppose they dead and they burning them,
supposing when some cane cutter
50 start chopping up snakes with a cutlass
he is severing the snake-armed god,
and suppose some hunter has caught
Hanuman in his mischief in a monkey cage.
Suppose all the gods were killed by electric light?

55 Sunset, a bonfire, roars in my ears;
embers of blown swallows dart and cry,
like women distracted,
around its cremation.
I ascend to my bed of sweet sandalwood.

DEREK WALCOTT
St Lucia

The Catherine Letter I

Strange   my writing to you

Can I say a cliché

Never thought I would see the day when you would cut me   glimpsed
you in   should have said at   should have said near   a bank one day; smile
waved; and you cut me

Catherine   name from the north

Well   there's a mystery to women of frost   the young men stride to the
woods and snip them dark lilacs   a wren wheels in the distance   the sun
shells east of the lake

Couples kiss in the field across the wild cherries

In the dream the woman is sitting under a cotton   a man kneels on the
slope   the pair meet in the mist, stuttering prayers

Have you seen lilies tilt in the wind

Do banks stretch shadows on people so that when they see the familiar
15 they turn away

Sometimes roses mistake violets for other flowers   Do you think there
will ever be concert between men and women   Catherine   sad   in
September

Some names sing in the air like lit swans

20 Catherine   name like a fir

The leaves turn with a fine cadence   The dancers touch hands under the
elms

Critic one   is this a letter or a poem

Critic two   surrealist nonsense

25 Critic three   language in dream sequence

I cry to the stones because I am lonely, the girl said to the dark

Perhaps if I look through this file I will find her charred letter

Catherine and Natalie, moving

The most beauteous virgin weeps in the rain

30 Catherine   if I talked to a fern do you think it would
answer   if I stopped at your window what

Hyacinths   I dial a number   soft click

A thrush glides in slow circles over the brook

Catherine stands by the fence, watching a leopard

35 I call you from fire   in the white wheel

I give you the valley

Tony McNeill

ANTHONY McNEILL
Jamaica

Letter

Dear Queen Elizabeth,
    Dear Queen, I take a long time since the last
    and am hoping you didn't mind;
    but, well, queen, I not sure how to start,
5 but something happening you should know.

    But your highness, I will start.

    As you know
    I coming every day
    to the libr'y by the square
10 and writing you.

    Well, the other day, I see this girl,
    working here,
    she new.
    And she tall, taller than me.
15 And she certain when she walk
    and she sure when she talk
    and I like she large
    ear-rings.

    And she face
20 and she hair
    making one
    from the front.

    From the side is a diff'rent thing.

    And she bam-bam!
25 moving quick
    tight and quick
    nutten loose. . .

    ent no use
        ent no use
30   ent no use
               dear queen elizabeth

    cos when she smile
    as she pass,
    as she pass
35 me dong here,
    nuffing I could do.

186

And she smile
all the time
every time I here.

40 I think she like me too.

And your highness
      how I want she!
Yes your highness
      is bad I need she!
45 And your highness
      is have I goin' have she!
          (sing) I and she goin' make some children
              de children goin' stand up tall tall
                an' when you goin' call dem niggah
50   dem ent goin' hear you at all!

And that is why dear Queen Elizabeth
I'm writing now to tell you
You could call off all the plans
To marry your daughter and me.

JOHN ROBERT LEE
St Lucia

Journey

When this journey begins
the hills around my city
are charred brown
are scarred black
5 where leaping yellow tongues
of flame are licking their way
through screaming tree crowns.

Not a single drop of rain
pierces that vice tight sky.
10 No water slakes my thirst.
Not even pundits cajoling gods
can alter this oven void.

My savannah is a dust bowl
her seared red skin
15 peeled singed dust choked

in a broiling wind.
My skin splits in the day
oozes a feverish secretion
night after stifling day.
20 Not even desire is fueled.

'I will not survive this drought'
is the name of the fear
rising from the depths anchoring
this razed
25 beaten
dazed
driven
voice that rasps crackling:
'This aridity is death.'

30 But
slowly
slowly
slowly
without a hint of haste
35 a terrible imbalance
restores itself.

One morning
a hawk thunders out
a cerulean high
40 feathered wings muscled taut.

Circling
Tightening the circle to the edge
of plummeting.
Circles once more
45 before gliding: an arrow
shafting its target.

Now this journey is sure
the hills around my city
are flushed green
50 are washed clean
breathing dewed buttercups
whose lips are raining
golden suns
gilding a flood of Ti Marie
55 whose pink pickered pickle flavour
hums.

Under my naked feet
roots roar
uttering leap saplings
60 resuscitating gnarled trunks
whose crowns are dripping lianas
down soaring valleys
rooted in solid bays
anchored in a frothing sea
65 pound
pound
pounding
another rejuvenation.

Where, you ask, this journey
70 leads?
It ain' matter.

Now I walk our streets
allied
communal
75 equally free
in the sluiced heat of the day
the rain charged wind of the night.

Down
down
80 down
that
long
long
arid tunnel
85 I
Prodigal
come to this flourishing sight
soaked in my island
stroked in her colours
90 reflecting her pools of resilient light.

RAOUL PANTIN
Trinidad and Tobago

Me Bredda

Oonoo call me bredda fi me!
Beg yuh tell him come yah quick!
Tell him bring him pelt-yuh-kin cow-cod
An bus-yuh open stick!

5   Me naw meck no joke wid yuh, mah!
Quick an brisk an pay me off,
Or ah call me bredda in yah
Meck him beat you till yuh sof!

Yuh answer me advertisment,
10   Yuh come slap a me yard
Come tell me how de pay is big
And how de work no hard.

Me never like yuh face, but when
Me bredda tell me seh
15   Dat yuh husban is a nice man
Mi decide fi come tedeh.

Me oversleep dis mornin, never
Wake till after eight.
Is a taxi-cab me teck come yah
20   Fi hinder me from late.

An now yuh start form fool bout yuh
No want me! What is dis!
Oonoo call me bredda fi me!
It naw go so, missis!

25   Yuh wi haffi beg me pardon loud
Meck all de neighbours hear!
Yuh wi haffi pay me two weeks
Wages, plus me taxi fare!

So ah talkin stupidness?
30   Oonoo call me bredda deh!
Ah-oh, yuh change yuh mine? Tank yuh.
Goodbye. Wha dat yuh seh?

Yuh would like fi know me bredda?
Me cyaan help yuh eena dat.
35   Me hooda like know him meself,
For is me one me parents got!

LOUISE BENNETT
Jamaica

190

Invocations

For the mysterious woman

I remember you
coming
hanging loose
toting invocations in a bag of cosmetic
5   medicine for blues
& in the transparency of night
shedding your celluloid skin
tempering my screams.
I remember you giving me baths
10   with water from Blue Basin
& your body scent like Ponds on varnished cedar softened
in the night heat by an oil lamp
flickering in my room's shadow
& oh yes
15   the sweetness of rain water we drank from
a calabash floating in the house bucket
& wash rag damp
to keep us dry.
I remember that style you spent years perfecting
20   down to that walk you sculptured from
pavement shadows
& oh, your surprises & superstitions
& the doorless walls you built around those special
mysterious things.

25   In my attempt to back-step up those tracks
to retrace their meanings, I end up with
mud on my shoe & fold
forgetting where the stepping stones we placed were left
striking match after match to find
30   that key we kept beneath the aloes plant
& fighting back maljo dogs hateful of strangers
for one more visit to
backrooms in backyards of backroads for
that special laughter that once brimmed over
35   with ideas

I remember your choir beauty from the early days
painted in the ever faint pastels
of that catholic glare
& those innocent eyes I saw through stained reflections
40   borne along the stations of the cross & marked pews
from which we were displaced from our worship by

privileged whispers
(*you were, even then, my most special virgin from the
        Legion of Mary*).
45 I remember you, drinking of the blood, eating
with yearning of the body, praising on high
sweet voices Et Gloria
(*You were my daughter of Fatima*)
& the romance of the bolero
50 & words to that song to which we danced
at the stroke of midnight still at the tip of my tongue.

These days
the best memories of yesterday
eye out only from static pages
55 like old photographs dying to come alive:
To breathe
To smell those raw, open smells
which intoxicated the air at night.
& even though everything seems so far out
60 of reach
I cling still to the desire
& charms of the past
to go arm in arm with you
up the back road where the asphalt ends

65 Through the tracks to the backyard
to concoct one more potion
in that mosquito nest from where we saw the sky
through holes in the roof of that quiet
leaning room
70 on the hill between Shangri La & Hell
before I face this city again

DAWAD PHILIP
Trinidad and Tobago

Lemonsong
For Moncada, and my son

In Cuba where something happened
in the province of Santiago, where something happened,
all roads climb to Moncada, where something happened.
That is why I am crying, my son,
5 under the cool leaves of the lemon trees.
There is a wound that will not heal,

like an eye
shut up, so
the glass will not spill a sheet
10 of tears down
shut up by dead men's hands, done men,
they hold its edges tight so
nothing can escape, the dreams
cannot fall away because of tears, the lemon leaves smelling faintly
15 of midday
in Santiago, in the shade
of your tomorrow.

The guide uses her hands
like a clock, marking the time
20 of the bullets:
     'The house is just as it was
     when they defended it'
And under that voice, the voices:
     'We need to sleep
25   under the ceiling of mouths
     who shout for freedom, all tongues
     the same
     they say
     we are here, we are here.'

30 I am crying under the lemon trees at Moncada
because of death and the hardness of such love.
Is this what we must pay
to be complete, my son?
Everything is so clean, so remembered.
35 Children sleep helplessly. You are a stranger.
I do not understand your innocence. The flesh
is a wound that will not heal;
I hold you together as though my hands would stop
the guide's hand
40 that makes holes in your side, in the house
as though I could keep you away
away from the choosing, as though I could
surround your calm.
They will teach you and take you away
45 they will make you a stranger.
What can I give you to fight?
Can we open no door
can we root no tree
can no house stand
50 without such sour sacrifice, without
the whisper of bullets in the hand?

I wait for you to wake
and be captured too
to be saved.
55 I am crying under the lemon trees at Moncada
because of their hard love, and the death they braved.

Today, Moncada. The pale, unchanging smell
of lemon trees. I make birds in your sleep
to walk among the serene leaves
60 as though the world were green for always
and nobody ever went away.
the colour of old uniforms.
                              They are
                              They fall, choked
65 by the smell of photographs: the young men
lying emptied, like guns
rusting against the rocks. They fall
through the holes in that back, that cheek, that eye,
everything, all so clean, so remembered.

70 I would take all the guns away, and melt them
to small bird shapes, gleaming behind glass,
and a man I know
who makes coffins too
would carve the wood
75 with pictures of quiet gardens, and we would go
for walks under the trees, and come home at night
to supper beside the cabinet, watching
the birds in their ironic flight.
            (They are falling like coins, like bullets, like soldiers
80   into the photographs
            of men who are done,
            who are dead, who desire
            only that we keep safe
            what they have won.
85   And what shall I desire for you, my son?)
I wrap them in sheets of secretly printed paper, reporting
the loss of lives, the growth of the Revolution.
I leave them beside the dead in the garden
under the turning shadow of the stones.
90 I am crying under the lemon trees at Moncada
because of their death, and the hardness of such love.

95   the white walls of the house,
                                    riddling:
    Is this how
    we earn time, with holes
    like old coins in a soldier's uniform?
100 The guide smoothes the air to the shape of a small hill,
    celebrating the victory of freedom, the silencing of death,
    the hardness of love that is greater than fear,
    the strength of young bone.

    I would try to tell you that
105 there are birds at Moncada,
    but the cool earth stops my mouth. You must make them
    yourself, you must want them.
    I would keep you asleep, but under the lids like glass
    in a small museum at Moncada
110 your eye is smooth, pressing the image, the stare
    of men who are dead, who are done, and the war
    is forever. I watch
    the window of your face
    and discover the price. The voices.
115 They are crying under the lemon trees at Moncada
    because of death and the hardness of their love.
         'The house is just
         as it was'
    and under, the voices:
120   'That the children be
         enduring as stones
         with the names of the dead cut
         into them.'

    Sleep until the gunfire wakes you
125 to a uniform the colour of lemon leaves.
    I rock you, solved,
    under a ceiling of mouths
    who have shouted for freedom.
    The tongues are different
130 but I recognise their love,
    they say
         'We are quiet. Awake.
         We are here, we are here.'

    Travelling like birds into your sleep.

DENNIS SCOTT
Jamaica

Signifying: Robber Talk

I am the Archipelago

I am the archipelago hope
Would mould into dominion; each hot green island
Buffetted, broken by the press of tides
And all the tales come mocking me
5 Out of the slave plantations where I grubbed
Yam and cane; where heat and hate sprawled down
Among the cane – my sister sired without
Love or law. In that gross bed was bred
The third estate of colour. And now
10 My language, history and my names are dead
And buried with my tribal soul. And now
I drown in the groundswell of poverty
No love will quell. I am the shanty town,
Banana, sugarcane and cotton man;
15 Economies are soldered with my sweat
Here, everywhere; in hate's dominion;
In Congo, Kenya, in free, unfree America.

I herd in my divided skin
Under a monomaniac sullen sun
20 Disnomia deep in artery and marrow.
I burn the tropic texture from my hair;
Marry the mongrel woman or the white;
Let my black spinster sisters tend the church,
Earn meagre wages, mate illegally,
25 Breed secret bastards, murder them in womb;
Their fate is written in unwritten law,
The vogue of colour hardened into custom
In the tradition of the slave plantation.
The cock, the totem of his craft, his luck,
30 The obeahman infects me to my heart
Although I wear my Jesus on my breast
And burn a holy candle for my saint.
I am a shaker and a shouter and a myal man;
My voodoo passion swings sweet chariots low.

35 My manhood died on the imperial wheels
That bound and ground too many generations;

From pain and terror and ignominy
I cower in the island of my skin,
The hot unhappy jungle of my spirit
40   Broken by my haunting foe my fear,
The jackal after centuries of subjection.
But now the intellect must outrun time
Out of my lost, through all man's future years,
Challenging Atalanta for my life,
45   To die or live a man in history,
My totem also on the human earth.
O drummers, fall to silence in my blood
You drum against the moon; break up the rhetoric
Of these poems I must speak. O seas,
50   O Trades, drive wrath from destinations.

ERIC ROACH
Trinidad and Tobago

My Song is for all Men

I
My song is for all men Jew Greek Russian
Communist pagan Christian Hindu Muslim Pole Parsee
And since my song is for all men
More than most I must state a case for the black man.

5   I have wandered with the Men of Devon over the Devon hills
Conned thought with Milton where low voices drift
through time buoying music over death and forgetfulness
I have wandered beyond to distant Caucasia
Skirting my wonder of blood wined in the beauty
10   Of green mountains hemmed by blue waters on Georgia's coast
I have listened to debate in London and Moscow
Prague Paris and many another town
I have heard statement confused or insistent
patient or fretted facing a claim
15   And ever the claim was the same
'This is my own' the voices repeated 'my hands have built it.
                    It is my very own. Show us your fruiting.'
Let me then bring mine own
This is mine own. I state a claim for the black man

20   I am the black man

I hide with pigmies in the hot depth of the forest that is Africa's
girdle
I am the Zulu striding hot storm over the brown whispering
veldt
25 that rides in my blood like a battle
I am the Ashanti I fold my strength in the beaten gold
of a stool shaped for immortals
I am the Nilotic standing one-legged for my rest
I am the Hyskos escaped out of Egypt and become king of
Ruandi
30 I am the miner baring the wealth of South Africa
I hold the fate of the world in my hands in the uranium pits of
the Congo
I am no more the man of Zambesi than I am the man of Limpopo
I am no less the man from the mountains of Kavirondo than I am
35 the warrior bred of the Masai
I am as much Ibo as I am Yoruba
I am all that is Africa I reach out to embrace those who have
left me
I dig cane-holes in hot West Indian islands
40 I run donkeyman on trampships plying from Cardiff
I wear a red cap on all North American railroad stations

I bring rough hands calloused in the tumult of weariness
Strong-boned not given to prayer force strained to hard bruis-
ing Bearing rough burdens to enrich men in England America
45 France Holland Brazil. I work for my bread.

A woman comes with me long-limbed high bosomed proud of
countenance
She walks abroad her presence dressed
Fluent of Earth and love
50 Sweet as the fresh-rained corn at early morning

Eyes soft as mountain lakes deep-shaded
O'er shot of sunshine truant midst the reeds
At hide and seek with laughter supply flung
The music of her motion

55 Sweeter is this purple grape
Than Pompadour's wild roses
Wide-eddied leaps life's promise
Strong
In the rivers of her keeping

60 The Black woman brings her beauty
I shall sing it
Bid every nation know
And worship it
With her at my side I measure all things
65 She is the source of my pride from her stem all my creations

II
And since there are those who pretend to estimate the peoples
Sum and divide them to suit the needs of their policy
That for this class, this for that superior nation,
Shaped and assessed on the rate of their own order in merit
70 There are some things I must say to them

And oh men of Europe Asia America and all the sea islands
Come near and look at these faces
For this also concerns you
75 And you men of Africa especially scan them well and remember
them

You will find them to-day
In London Paris New York Buenos Aires Madrid and Berlin
One and all for themselves very superior persons
The Bitch of Belsen too was a very superior person
80 She was for herself a fine humanist held a peculiar conception
Of art, she loved dogs had a taste highly refined above others
for parchment
The skin of a painter musician a giant tattooed
Some poet greater than these to sing the strength of the peoples
85 Alone could suffice her for lampshades
She too shared our shape
She knew her man carnally kissed him caressed him longed for
him utterly when the need was upon her
As would a bitch for her dog? no she was at every point woman
90 And around herself and her living she wore a beastly deception

There are many like her in our world let us never forget them
Let us examine them
Swear with me here an oath that these will no longer govern our
world

95 These are the men who find my presence constraining in Alabama
Barbados London Texas and similar places
They teach their children to turn their faces away when they see
me

199

They say my features are coarse and repulsive
100 Too like the ape for man. Against these I have always to argue
my humanity

I may not travel in cabins on shipboard with them
Nor sit at table with them command them in armies or navies
in churches pray with them or for them
105 In Johannesburg their child if his skin be white
May push me from his path on the sidewalk
And as he feels his strength increasing to manhood
He may kick me into the gutter. No law brings me redress
They would have me stand in their polity one for whom laws are
110 made not one who may make them
My part to obey and to serve hew wood and draw water
I am expected to stand respectfully bared while this kind talk to
me
Crawl cringe and dance like a poodle trained to beg crusts or a
115 bone for amusement
At Martinsville in the United States of America they hanged me
on the word of a white prostitute hot from the stews
Where all night long she fretted her pennies
Prone till the morning taught her lost virtue
120 The source of its pride when she saw me
No one could prove my guilt there was none to be proven
The judge simply stated my death would have a wholesome effect
on the community
So they burnt me at Richmond in the name of Christ and
125 democracy
To smother the fears that shook them as they played at a race
of the masters

To all my wide continent I welcomed these they came to Africa
seized all they could lay hands upon
130 Took the best lands for their tilling to build them white houses
I pass them each day cool deep-shaded in green
Their dwelling places wanton in loveliness
Spread for their senses by sky river and sea

I shelter my weariness in old packing cases
135 Cast of their luxury offscourings of cardboard and tin
Scraped of their surfeit too mean to cover their dog
My nakedness is whipped from sleep by rain pouring
at midnight to strip me in torment the last space
Earth pledged safe from their craving
140 To these I have something to say

200

These you claim are only my just deservings
Rags and old packing cases fair receivings
For beasts such as I am so you say
Crabbed you would tent me manacled as madmen
145 Once crouched beneath your palaces

I am unlearned in philosophies of government
I may not govern myself children must learn of their elders
till they are elders themselves
I know nothing of science never created a great civilisation
150 Poetry song music sculpture are alike foreign to my conceiving

I have never built a monument higher than a mudhut
Nor woven a covering for my body other than the passing leaves
of the grass
I am the subman
155 My footprints are nowhere in history

This is your statement, remember, this your assessment
I merely repeat you
Remember this too, I do not ask you to pity me
Remember this always you cannot condescend to me

160 There are many other things I remember and would have you
remember as well
I smelted iron in Nubia when your generations still ploughed
with hardwood
I cast in bronze at Benin when London was marshland
165 I built Timbuctoo and made it a refuge for learning
When in the choirs of Oxford unlettered monks shivered
unwashed

My faith in the living mounts like a flame in my story
I am Khama the Great
170 I helped Bolivar enfranchise the Americas
I am Omar and his thousands who brought Spain the light of
the Prophet
I stood with my spear among the ranks of the Prempehs
And drove you far from Kumasi for more than a century
175 I kept you out of my coasts and not the mosquitoes
I have won many bitter battles against you and shall win them
again
I am Toussaint who taught France there was no limit to liberty
I am Harriet Tubman flouting your torture to assert my faith in
180 man's freedom
I am Nat Turner whose daring and strength always defied you

I have my yesterdays and shall open the future widely before me

I am Paul Robeson
I send out my voice and fold peoples warmly to my bosom
185 I sow courage in myriad bleak places where it is grown worn
My song kept this fire alight in the fiords of Norway under the
Nazis

for my power is never diminished
I pile volcanoes in the minds of Mississipi sharecroppers
190 I engage continents
Beyond all bars you set I shall reach out
To tear life's glory down I shall reach out
To set life's crown upon mine own head with mine own hand
Shall reach out and never forget the reckoning

195 But first I must separate myself from your every particular
I must touch you at no point
I must shun your very fringes
And in all my living I shall never be alone.

PETER BLACKMAN
Barbados

The Red Robber

From the depths of burning Hell
I came
Cast out because I raped Satan's daughter
My rage is a millionfold
5 My mother was a dragon
And my father a Griffin
I can drink a river
And belch an ocean
When my name is called in vain
10 My belly blows rain
Flooding villages, towns and cities
I eat countries boiled in vinegar
Emperors and kings tremble
At the sound of my name
15 Snakes hiss! wolves howl!
Volcanoes split fire exploding
Damnation scattering the sun
Watch me

As I devour these islands
20 Watch me
As I drink the Caribbean sea
Brain-washing minds hatched
From a rotten egg circling
The plague-ridden universe
25 I was the conqueror, slave-driver
And slave
My body grew in the passing
Of centuries
I can destroy
30 And I can create
Watch me
Reshaping islands from sea-spray
Sweat and grass.

FAUSTIN CHARLES
Trinidad and Tobago

Nigger Sweat

'Please have your passport and all documents out and ready
for your interview. Kindly keep them dry' – *Notice in
Waiting-room, US Embassy, Visa Section, Kingston, 1983*

No disrespect, mi boss,
just honest nigger sweat;
well almost, for is true
some of we trying to fool you
5 so we can lose weself
on the Big R ranch
to find a little life;
but, boss, is hard times
make it, and not because
10 black people born wutliss:
so, boss, excuse this nigger sweat.
And I know that you know it
as well as me,
this river running through history
15 this historical fact, this sweat
that put the aroma
in your choice Virginia
that sweeten the cane
and make the cotton shine;

203

20   and sometimes I dream a nightmare dream
that the river rising, rising
and swelling the sea and I see
you choking and drowning
in a sea of black man sweat
25   and I wake up shaking
with shame and remorse
for my mother did teach me,
Child, don't study revenge.
Don't think we not grateful, boss,
30   how you cool down the place for we comfort,
but the line shuffle forward
one step at a time
like Big Fraid hold we,
and the cool-cut, crew-cut Marine boy
35   wid him ice-blue eye and him walkie-talkie
dissa walk through the place and pretend
him no see we.
But a bring mi handkerchief,
mi mother did bring me up right,
40   and, God willing, I keeping things cool
till we meet face to face,
and a promise you, boss,
if I get through I gone,
gone from this bruk-spirit, kiss-me-arse place.

EDWARD BAUGH
Jamaica

Me As Well – The Blackman

Child of the self-conscious
I remake the mind
In my own image;
        This is my time.

5   I am the black child of history
Migratory through centuries.

Who said: 'To liberate the Indian
Is to free a continent?'
Spoke for other men than me;
10   Though I am of the same tree,
With roots in three geographies.

I am neither whiteman,
                    Nor yellowman,
Though all nurtured my resting place
15 And fecunded the bloodstream.

But the black stream
Could not clarify the stench
Of humanism cluttered in blood
Sodden in the soiled paper
20 Europe posited to my past.

Nations I slaved to build,
When I rebelled to make men
Aware of my manhood,
Turned faces in forgetfulness.

25 For all I was the thing
                    in history –
the barbaric; the semi-barbaric; the savage
                    that was me.

Or so they said of me to me
30 Till I plunged into my past
                    and theirs
The skeletons were sad to see.

The vision was the self-righteous prism
Of Europe's narcissism.

35 For all who cross fertilised
That are chained in this prison
            I paint this picture:

To free a continent
We liberate not only Indian
40   and workman
But me as well – the blackman

JOHN LA ROSE
Trinidad and Tobago

Weroon Weroon

I came to a benab
sharpening my arrow of stone
knitting my hammock of air
tying my feathers all around my head.

5 Then I drank from the calabash of my ancestors
and danced my dance of fire
Weroon Weroon –
Land of the waters flowing over me
Weroon Weroon

10 I prayed to the blue ocean of heaven
dreaming of the voyage of death
and my corial of paradise paddling forever.

Now I climb toward the hole of heaven
and my hands are stretched to the altar of god
15 O wonder of all the stars departed
Weroon Weroon Weroon. . .

MARTIN CARTER
Guyana

Epilogue. 1976

and then you came
you stood
between the sunset
and the night
5 but neither felt the wind
the rain
nor seized the time
to contemplate
that distant thunder
10 you came
I searched
the hollow fissures
of the dark
but nothing moved
15 all through the empty hours
nothing stirred
I stopped a dream

and touched
the wounded night
20 is there no life
no leap
no gain

the mountain mocks
the plain
25 proud rocks
decay
night never knows
the day
I feel no pain
30 no hate
no shame
nobody knows my name.

LESTER EFEBO WILKINSON
    Trinidad and Tobago

Wreck

Jack of all spades, mastered by none
steered between ole mas' and half-mast
I cursed to my heart's contempt
needled by rhetoric, carded
for the treadmill, I follower
flounder

Sell
my frenzy to the Trade Winds
my beating
10 memory of the doldrums
and watch life's storm settle in
a teacup.

No politician,
I cannot
15 harbour hate
take your thorny existence
and bramble with your faith;
I will return to the cupped breast.

Hemmed in by silence
20 I skirt the pain
as this ruled life inches along
my palms
lined with the fronds'
reflection measured to
25 a tropical breeze,

Like a spider's seamy web.

My vision beached to a stare,
dogged
by the flea-bite of fear.

30 Hitting the bottle my faith splinters.

VICTOR QUESTEL
Trinidad and Tobago

Praise Songs, Prayers, and Incantations

Ave Maria

From a church across the street
    Children repeat
Hail Mary, full of Grace;
Skipping the syllables, Follow-the-Leader pace.

5 A little girl (the Lord is with Thee),
    White in organdy,
Lifts her starched, black face
    Towards the barricaded altar
Meadowed in lace.

10 (Blessed art Thou among women.)
    Her child's fingers string the coloured beads
One after one.
(Blessed is the fruit of Thy womb);
Yea, and blessed, too, ripe fruit on tree window-
15   close,
    Under a tropical sun.

Bend low the laden bough
    Child-high; sweeten her incense-flavoured breath
With food, good Mary. (Holy Mary, Mother of God,
20 Pray for us sinners.) And for the blameless –
    Now, before the hour of their death.

BARBARA FERLAND
Jamaica

Litany

I hold the splendid daylight in my hands
Inwardly grateful for a lovely day.
Thank you life.
Daylight like a fine fan spread from my hands
5 Daylight like scarlet poinsettia

Daylight like yellow cassia flowers
Daylight like clean water
Daylight like green cacti
Daylight like sea sparkling with white horses
10 Daylight like sunstrained blue sky
Daylight like tropic hills
Daylight like a sacrament in my hands.
Amen.

GEORGE CAMPBELL
Jamaica

Malefactor (*Left*)

So you is God?
Den teck wi down! Tiefin doan bad
like crucifyin!
Wha do you, man?
5 Save all a wi from dyin!

Malefactor (*Right*)

Doan bodder widdim, Master; him
must die;
but when you kingdom come, remember I.
When you sail across de sea,
5 O God of Judah, carry I wit dee.

MERVYN MORRIS
Jamaica

Guard-ring

Moon shadow burning,
Watch where I walking, Lord.
Make mi foot step hard
on the enemy's shadow
5 an hear me.
        I wearing de ring dem tonight –
one gainst hate and de red pepper
tongue of malice, a snake-eye
bone-ring to touch
10 if I buck up de tempter,

one ring gainst love-me
an one gainst de finger of famine,
an one for the death by drowning,
an one from fire;
15 an a bright copper ring
that I fine a in a fish belly,
tun me safe an salt
from de barracuta teet of desire.

But moon shadow falling.
20 I fraid for de shape of de winding –
de road too crooked,
it making a rope to twine me!
An Lord, I tired
to tell yu mi torment, but listen
25 an learn me, an reach me
to home.   I believe
in de blessed ring, but Chris'
I praising yu candle also,
I raising mi heart like a smalls,
30 like a coal that outing
to light it –
              guard me asleep an awake!
De ring did bless in de balm yard
but Thee I praise.
35 I singing out loud
for de hill dem to hear me an tremble

De Lord is my Shepherd,
I shall not fear!
I singing so loud, down to de moon
40 going shake, I crying out,
Chris' yu hear!
An de moonshine wetting mi face up
like oil of plenty.

I going alone to mi house
45 wid de ring pon mi finger,
but walk wid me ever
an ever, tree score an ten,
and de moon shall wet me,
de ring shall praise Thee an heal me
50 an de mout shall bless Thee
for ever, amen
Amen.

DENNIS SCOTT
Jamaica

211

The Obstacle Course

Poor sons:
grant them wings.
They who need to run
To climb trees
5   climb mountains
    climb out
Grant them capes that vanish
when reality be hot on their heels
They who must slip minds
10   & the
                             chain of events
                           inherited.

They who must dodge
time.

15 Black boys
grant them wings on their sneakers
to get through alleys
                   o
                    v
20   e
                       r
                        w
                         a
                          l
25   l
                            l
                              s
                             & across roofs:

They who need be faster then
speeding bullets
30   when chased
                      to be
eliminated.

Poor son.
Another runner was stopped last night
35 at 16.
Tired. Aged.
Panting a pool of blood
a burning hole in his chest
screaming for a fan
40 giving up the fleet. . .brought to a raging rest.

The screeching siren
        swirling night amber
against a sea of black
a moon red
45 poor sons
poor sons
grant that they be swift
with wings forever.

DAWAD PHILIP
Trinidad and Tobago

Petit Careme

This year again
the drought
too long this sun
scorched rock
5 this time
too long this life
is only heat lord
only heat lord

Bury mih down
10 in the hot
Manza sand
near the chip-chip
too much steam lord
and the nights lord
15 fuss they bright lord
dem silent nights
eh holy nights no more
too much hate lord
all dem guns lord
20 bawling through the mid-night
dem is Gods lord
see dem flame lord
too much pain lord
too much pain lord

25 So burn mih, bredda!
waste mih crooked life
with yuh red hot irons, man.
rip loose mih flesh

with yuh flame-warm seed
30   is you who reap mih sweat
now rape mih soul.

only heat lord.
rain done gone
and wind blowing warm
35   real warm
this petit careme.

LESTER EFEBO WILKINSON
Trinidad and Tobago

December 1974: a Lament

And the euphorbia,
Snow on its branches, Lord.
Though our sun melts flesh,
The euphorbia whitens.
5   The year is dying.
My time is dying.
What have I planted, Lord?

And the poinsettia,
Blood stars the hedges, Lord,
10   Daytime and startime
The red spears cluster.
My year is dying.
My cry dies.
What have I planted, Lord?

15   And gungu also,
Pods weighting the branches, Lord,
Though Your children are poor.
(Cry thanks for fit food).
My year is dying, dying,
20   And blood runs thin.
What have I planted, Lord?

I cannot afford
Time's waste, fruit-
less sweat, point-
25   less talk. For time points.
And spears of poinsettia threaten.

Wasting I cannot afford.
Drive me to plant, Lord!

Grand trees I cannot afford.
30 The quick crops, Lord!
Ambition I cannot afford.
The cash crops, Lord!

SLADE HOPKINSON
Guyana

For Roberta Flack & Sisters

Black voice sing our new poetry.
Far off now, refined anguish oozing
from alexandrines, smothered in iambic
pentameters. Your words astride the music,
5 singing under skin 'Love me baby.'

Closed off by day, bossed by traffic
we forget. such release now, aural bridge
quickens, in a quiet room
grey mind, translucent nerves
10 journey to a half-remembered place.
A time when the drum under leaves,
flute over red savannah played
our cells into life.

There is a loneliness and sadness
15 between us black lovers. We are
of your poem, in your music yet,
we want to make together the poem
of your voice,
the breath of your pain.

20 Witness with us now, you
give the first reed, help us
to take hold, help us
to plait
the past
25 into our future.

CHRISTINE CRAIG
Jamaica

For Angela Davis

Rain blazes in that hemisphere
of my mind
where little else happens
neither sunshine nor cloudburst
5 and certainly not the blossoming of the
power of love you cherish
which so much overwhelms my tongue
given to speech
in the necessary workplaces
10 where freedom is obscene.

And from a drab window falls the
happy consequence of clouds
which the roots of passionate trees
receive with splendid gratitude
15 and which may return to us all in
their time
and in their special ways,
linking hand to fruit
and fruit to the promise of our
20 prayerful hope and love
and the triumph of the effort of
the always beating pulse
in the wrist and temple of the architect
who wars.
25 I am thinking about you,
Angela Davis
I am thinking about you and
what I want to do
is to command the drying pools
30 of rain
to wet your tired feet and
lift your face
to the gift of the roof of
clouds we owe you.

MARTIN CARTER
Guyana

Pilar

Pilar
stands, small thin feet flat
on the sand, laughing with
her small, thin body and hands
5 clutched at her side.
Pilar
runs, slightly up on her toes
down the narrow corridor past
the white bathroom on the right,
10 into her yellow room.
Pilar
cries, cunning in her screams,
one eye on your surrender to
her infant rebellion. She knows
15 you cannot resist.
Pilar
loves, her hands cupped as they
touch your face, her blue-grey
eyes seeing you through, seeing
20 you do, seeing you.
Pilar
sleeps, busy head tossed back-
wards, small frail body flung
everywhere; dreams perhaps of
25 intangible worlds.
Pilar
I gave you nothing but a name,
a wild, imaginary vision; the
straddling of three continents.
35 The fulfillment of my tribe.

RAOUL PANTIN
Trinidad and Tobago

217

Song of Praise

Praise the Lord in all things coming,
Praise the Lord walking or running.

When dragons drool near your head,
Praise the Lord.
5 When hot harmattan winds crease your face,
Praise the Lord.
When your dream vanishes wide and empty,
Praise the Lord.
When sorrows come on full and plenty,
10 Praise the Lord.

Praise the Lord in all things coming,
Praise the Lord walking or running.

When a thousand chains enfold your body,
Praise the Lord.
15 When by love, they melt and you feel happy,
Praise the Lord.
When ambitions fall,
Man, rise up again and praise the Lord;
Man, rise up again and praise the Lord.

20 You see 12–headed monsters staring you down,
Praise the Lord.
You see the pathways increasing with snakes,
Praise the Lord.
They assume shapes like human beings,
25 They call you names behind your back;
They pull at your hair,
Try to knot-up your legs,
Try to knot-up your hands
Try to knot-up your head.

30 Still, you must praise the Lord in all things
coming;
Praise the Lord walking or running.

I say, praise the Lord in all things coming,
Praise the Lord walking or running.

TONY KELLMAN
Barbados

Mother the Great Stones Got to Move

Mother, one stone is wedged across the hole in our history
and sealed with blood wax.
In this hole is our side of the story, exact figures,
headcounts, burial artefacts, documents, lists, maps
5 showing our way up through the stars; lockets of brass
containing all textures of hair clippings.
It is the half that has never been told, some of us
must tell it.

Mother there is the stone on the hearts of some women and men
10 something like an onyx, cabochon cut
which hung on the wearer seeds bad dreams, speaking for the small
dreamers of this earth, plagued with nightmares, yearning
for healing dreams
We want that stone to move.

15 Upon an evening like this mother, when one year is making way
for another, in a ceremony attended by a show of silver stars,
mothers see the moon, milk-fed, herself a nursing mother
and we think of our children and the stones upon their future
and we want these stones to move.

20 For the year going out came in fat at first
but towards the harvest it grew lean.
And many mouth corners gathered white
and another kind of poison, powdered white
was brought in to replace what was green.
25 And death sells it with one hand
and with the other death palms a gun
then death, gets death's picture
in the papers asking,
'Where does all this death come from?'
30 Mother, stones are pillows
for the homeless sleep on concrete sheets.
Stone flavours soup, stone is now meat
the hard-hearted giving our children
stones to eat.

35 Mother the great stones over mankind got to move.
It's been ten thousand years we've been watching them now
from various points in the universe.
From the time of our birth as points of light
in the eternal coiled workings of the cosmos.
40 Roll away stone of poisoned powders come

to blot out the hope of our young.
Move stone of sacrificial lives we breed
to feed up tribalistic economic machines.
From across the pathway to mount morning
45 site of the rose quartz fountain
brimming anise and star water
bright fragrant for our children's future.

Mother these great stones got to move.

LORNA GOODISON
Jamaica

Tracing, Curses and
other Warnings

Cuss-Cuss

Gwan, gal, yuh favour teggereg!
Ah weh yuh gwine go do?
Yuh an yuh boogooyagga frien-dem
Tink me fraid a yuh?

5 Go weh, yuh favour heng-pon-nail!
Is me yuh waan fi trace?
Me is jus de one fi teck me han
An leggo pon yuh face.

Fi-me had no jine chuch, an me naw
10 Pay licen fi me mout.
Me wi tell yuh bout yuh – see yah,
Gal, no bodder get me out!

Me no know is what kine a chuch
Fi-yuh mout coulda jine –
15 Yuh lip-dem heng dung lacka when
Mule cyaan meck up him mine.

Gwan! Me an yuh no combolo –
Yuh foot shapeless an lang
Like smaddy stan far fling dem awn
20 An meck dem heng awn wrang!

Fi-yuh foot favour capital K!
Koo pon yuh two nose-hole –
Dem dis big an open out like
Miss Jane outsize fish bowl.

25 Go weh! Yuh cyaan bwile sof egg
But still yuh waan get ring –
No man na gwine fi married yuh
When yuh cyaan do a ting.

Is grudge yuh grudgeful! Me cyaan cook
30 But me ben go dah good school –
Me got intelligency, yuh
Illiterated fool!

Me sorry fi de man yuh get –
De po ting hooden nyam
35 When yuh ackebus him salt-fish
An bwilivous him yam.

LOUISE BENNETT
Jamaica

A Midnight Woman to the Bobby

No palm me up, you dutty brute,
You' jam mout' mash like ripe bread-fruit;
You fas'n now, but wait lee ya,
I'll see you grunt under de law.

5 You t'ink you wise, but we wi' see;
You not de fus' one fas' wid me;
I'll lib fe see dem tu'n you out,
As sure as you got dat mash' mout'.

I born right do'n beneat' de clack
10 (You ugly brute, you tu'n you' back?)
Don' t'ink dat I'm a come-aroun',
I born right 'way in 'panish Town.

Care how you try, you caan' do mo'
Dan many dat was hyah befo';
15 Yet whe' dey all o' dem te-day?
De buccra dem no kick dem 'way?

Ko 'pon you' jam samplatta nose:
'Cos you wear Mis'r Koshaw clo'es
You t'ink say you's de only man,
20 Yet fus' time ko how you be'n 'tan.

You big an' ugly ole tu'n-foot
Be'n neber know fe wear a boot;
An' chigger nyam you' tumpa toe,
Till nit full i' like herrin' roe.

25 You come from mountain naked-'kin,
     An' Lard a mussy! you be'n thin,
     For all de bread-fruit dem be'n done,
     Bein' 'poil' up by de tearin' sun:

     De coco couldn' bear at all,
30 For, Lard! de groun' was pure white-marl;
     An' t'rough de rain part o' de year
     De mango tree dem couldn' bear.

     An' when de pinch o' time you feel
     A 'pur you a you' chigger heel,
35 You lef' you' district, big an' coarse,
     An' come join buccra Police Force.

     An' now you don't wait fe you' glass,
     But trouble me wid you' jam fas';
     But wait, me frien', you' day wi' come,
40 I'll see you go same lak a some.

     Say wha'? – 'res' me? – you go to hell!
     You t'ink Judge don't know unno well?
     You t'ink him gwin' go sentance me
     Widout a soul fe witness i'?

CLAUDE McKAY
Jamaica

With Respect

     You stop red man or you done
     Cause if you en stop carry on
     An' if you done you better wipe
     Cause I don't want to carry on smellin'
5 Dat material dat you just been spittin'.
     Yuh talk up talk roun talk down
     Yuh rave, yuh rage an' yuh stray
     'Cause when I put all o' da talk in de pot
     It boil down to idiotic scientific
10 Good white and good black bring good red man?
     But human doan work by arithmetic
     If you en know dat yet boy yuh sick.

     Now to put a few little things straight,
     I en suck my teet at you chief

15 'Cause a no-teet man can' suck teet
I chupse and chupsin' is a privilege
For evah West Indian rich or poor,
And doan fuget Mr Pompasset
Dem is chupses, stupses and chupses.

20 Den yuh call me a so an' so baboon!
Not a ting en wrong wid dat
All 'o we is some sort o 'oon
Quadroon tycoon or racoon, so
Doan bus' you balloon Mr Coon.

25 But some o' what you say got in trut'
Cause whuh in de ol' goat in de Kiddy.

You talk like you muddah did a Hottentot
But I cross Hottentot an' Ashanti,
Low fire does boil up me blood
30 An' chief science save me life twice
Spaniard man in Cuba get vex
An' fly fuh he gun to mobilise muh,
One twis' o' de wris' pon 'de ockya
An' e han' done knucka in de holster,
35 You lucky I en had it hay wid muh
Wid de best respects uh woulda lick yuh
Anyhow wuh en ketch yuh en pass yuh.

Yuh got some good good stan' pipe argument
Africa fuh black, English fuh
40 White, West Indies fuh brown
So you kind ought to boss all de town?
Yuh know yuh right yuh right Mr Houseclear
But family to mule is wunnah fault
Mule does cock up an' kick up but doan breed
45 An' to boss would mean 'nough mulatto,
But jackass en altogether ass
Cause horse and mule is minority
So you wasting yuh breath Mr Pawgee
Unless yuh did airin' yuh mout'
50 But why you doan try Jeyes fluid
An flush out yuh Bread and Cheese vault?

You sorry enough slavery done
De Limey let wunnah keep slave too
An' wunnah show de white Massa a trick or two
55 How yuh like now to stir up uh ants'nest
An' bade muh in a tayche o' molasses
Den nail muh by me ear to a bully tree

An leggo de ants pun muh body,
Den light some dry twigs an sour grass
60 An cook me slow till uh soft
Den grig me to see if uh done
An' call yuh sooners fuh roast nigguh
Dem did good ol' days Mr Ecky.

Wunna sweet skin bucky tantalise
65 Poor niggy mashitate 'e and squlch 'e,
Put 'e in a stranna and call um
Civilise! Uhunh, brutalise
Is civilise, Mr Shanna Foot Tusheet?
Too sorry all yuh kin do is fire muh
70 But I kin fire you too Mr Sugar Cake
An' you en got nuh Union fuh put yuh back.
Um is fire fuh fire nowadays Jack
Illegal or legal fire fire does bu'n
So tek muh talk wid respects
75 An swallow yuh gal yuh red wretch
Tank de Lord fuh witness and me mash mout
Tank de Lord de ockya tekkin' a rest
Or de butts and de bites and de licks
Would mek yuh tink dat flat-han'-dildoe is
                                        flanellette,
80 An de missy would be 'nointin' yuh ass til
                                        Nebruary mornin'.

BRUCE ST JOHN
Barbados

Cherries

I

So when the hammers of the witnesses of heaven are raised all
    together
up yonder

there will be dumbness in the choir tonight

5 when the voices are raised all together
black kites flying on what should be a holiday

there will be silence in the cathedral

a woman loves a man

she will lick the sweat from his forehead
10 she will walk miles to see him
and wait for him by the corner

she will bear his children loudly

upon the earth is firm foot
toes searching the top-soil
15 gripping

the instep, the angles of knub, heel and ankle
are grey with the roads
with the long hypodermics of noon

the dress tucks itself over the black buttocks
20 into the suction of thighs
the hip is a scythe
grass growling along the hillside

she will bend forward with the hoe: *huh*
and the gravel will answer her: *so*

25 she will swing upward with the hoe: *huh*
and the bones of the plantation will come ringing to meet her: *so*
her sweat will water the onions and the shaddock and the wild
thyme

she will bear his children proudly

30 but when he turns sour on her
scowling, wiping her face with his anger
stiffening his spine beside her on the bed
not caressing her curves with eye-

lash or word or jook of the elbow
35 she will curdle like milk
the bones of the plantation will come ringing to meet her: *so*
the bucket will rattle in the morning at the stan'pipe

but there will be no water
the skillet will rattle at midday
40 but there will be no milk
she will become the mother of bastards

II

when the hammers are raised all together
rows of iron teeth swinging down: *huh*

there will be dumbness in the choir tonight

45 when the voices are raised all together
black fists gathering storm on what is not
a holiday

there will be silence in the cathedral

the light will fall through pains of glass
50 on broken stone

on steps that can go no farther
on love alive bleeding on its thorns

when a woman loves a man
when a man naddent

III

55 if there are ways of saying yes
i do not know them

if there are dreams
i cannot recall them to the light

if there is rage
60 it is cool cinder

in the heat of the day
i swear i will sweat no more

knife, bill-hook, sweet bramble
i will burn in my bush of screams

65 hoe: i will work
        root, mud, marl, burden

needle: i will sew
        thread, stitch, embroidered image

jesus: i will serve thee

70 knee, copper, rain falling from heaviest heaven of storm

but i will drink you no more
touch you no more
sweaten you out on the lumps of the mattress no longer

the hoe will stand in the corner by the backdoor
75 cane flowers will flicker with rainflies
but there will be no crop-over songs

the fields will grow green soundlessly
the roots will fatten until they burst
and then they will fatten again until they burst

80 but there will be no kukoo or okro or jug

the needle will grow rusty in the cloth:
pin, pinch of thread, thimble:
it will make no silver track and tremble far into the night

no dress will take shape over my head
85 slipping down like water over my naked breasts

the seats of the chapel will remain empty
the wicks burning at altar till daybreak
fattened by shadows and moths

your foetus i will poison
90 dark dark mollusc
spinach, susum, suck-de-well-dry bush

the child still fish, still lizard,
wrinkled gill and croaking gizzard

i will destroy: blinding the eyeballs
95 pulling out the flag of its tongue by the shreds
ripping open the egg of its skull with sunless manchioneal
blisters

i will carry the wet twitching rag
bearing your face, conveying your futureless race
in its burst bag of balls to your doorstep

100 *maaaa:* it will cry
and the windows will be pulled down tight against the wind

228

meeowww: it will howl
and a black dog will go prowling past the dripping pit latrines

and when the moon is a wild
105 flower falling through cloud, from patch to shade you will see it

once our child, our toil of touch, our sharing
sitting under the sandbox tree, smiling smiling

sipping its plate of bleed

IV

these images of love i leave you
110 when i no longer need you

man, manwart, manimal

EDWARD KAMAU BRATHWAITE
Barbados

Last Lines

This is the last line I draw.
Alright. Draw the last line.
But I tell you, yonder
is a next. No line never last
5 no death not forever.
You see this place   You see it?
All of it? Watch it good.
Not a jot nor a tittle
going lost. Every old
10 twist-up man you see,
every hang-breast woman,
every bang-belly pickney,
every young warrior
who head wrinch
15 with weed, white powder
black powder or indeed
the very vile persuasion
of the devil (for him
not bedridden, you know)
20 every small gal-turn-ooman
that you crucify on the

cross of your sex
before her like naseberry
start sweeten.
25 I swear to you
every last one shall live.
Draw therefore, O governor,
prime minister, parson,
teacher, shopkeeper,
30 politician, university lecturer,
resonant revolutionaries,
draw carefully that
last fine line
of your responsibility.

PAMELA MORDECAI
Jamaica

Cadence

The sound of silence
is the sound of fear
is the empty sound
of this steel pan-ic
5 orchestration.
Oh listen to that cadence
of suspense of suspicion
and pause suspended
while the maestro massa
10 with arms upraised
freezes the status quo.

The silence of death
outwaves the microwaves
and would be conductors
15 of this unfinished
symphony
are shushed
and shewed and silenced.

The steel pan-ic players
20 wait in panic for the rest
of the score, in panic they wait
the last panoramic seconds
as their lives float fleetingly

before them and a vision
25 of the silence of fear
evokes a cadenza that is a dirge
or a swansong of liberty.

Drain. Drain brain drain.
We are down the sluice
30 of your slimy passage
where the stench of your deeds
your dying, assails the sensitivity,
and there is no forgiveness
only regret for sins
35 of omission and commission;
stem not the flow of your life blood
of ideas and loyalty and patriotism
by false promises and imprisonment.

I go. I go on the dolorous search
40 for dollars, a jew I go
to wander lost and homeless
(but stinking rich)
for my heart is torn out
by the roots and I feel no pain.

45 Continue your score. The cadence lengthens
and posterity is your audience.
Down comes the hand of the massa
conductor – no sound; the players
panic; then cacophany, horrible
50 sounds, as pebbles pelted
on a roof, notes roll from the tarnished
instruments and are tossed
by the tympani.
Minims, crotchets, quavers
55 of liberty quaver
and disappear
                    down
                        drains.

ANSON GONZALEZ
Trinidad and Tobago

231

Trini

I have heard you, Trini,
Seen you head down paths
On shores of sand
Where tides erased your footprints
5 Even as you walked.

I have heard you, brother,
Listened to your songs of rice-mud parodies
The beat of cocoa-trance
The lance of coffee-heated perfumes
10 Drying on your sweat,
The salt of seas of fevered, quailing sun
The wicked fun of small, unmarketable catch,
I have heard your voice.

You friend, without some epic past
15 To cling on to, some tale to tell the sons,
Except that those who came had thought
Their tasks would weave you one,
But left you only rituals, flayed hopes;
And now you've learnt
20 To spend your time
Creating dreams, beneath the slime
The dust of scholar's chalk,
Hoping that book will stork
The clarifying odes.

25 But look now, brother, friend, observe
On evenings when the sun lends sky
Its miraged miracles, hued flames of gold,
How tame the sea becomes
How soft the world, subdued by change
30 Melts like a child, mothered by awesome innocence.
Remember too, on flaking dawns
How sober kiskidees proclaim their gloried
Prophesies of sunny day, the joys,
While sacred cedar scents summon the breath,
35 How blest is waking.

Nature herself hides not
In past or ink-lit parables,
Seeks not her truths
In memory or dream,

40 Take heed, Trini,
    The place to find yourself
    Is in that silent, sacred spring
    Which sings within the love inspired heart,

    And time Trini,
45 Is now.

SELWYN BHAJAN
Trinidad and Tobago

Mammon

    ghost, guardian-spirit of banks, trans-national corporations,
    daylight deals in air-conditioned sewers
    ghoul, eating the flesh of our dead childhood
    ghost, effluvium of the rotting innocence in the skull-vault
5   ghost, smoke-screen between my self and your self
    whose language is a hissing yes to vice
    who salivates hypocrisies and sleeks the tongue with moss
    who slithers between Man and Woman
    who multiplies us only to divide
10 who adds and then subtracts to zero
    ghost, slick as night-wet city streets
    vinyl-skinned and glittering with devices
    whose rock-pit is a gold-mine near Johannesburg
    mammon
15 watching our children growing
    never-closing nickel eyes minting their images
    watch him, this god
    rattle like dice, like thirty pieces of silver
    watch him
20 flick and rustle a green promising tongue
    grin like a wallet opening
    watch him
    whispering to you now.

KENDEL HIPPOLYTE
Jamaica

The Country Black Black

But how tonight Black so?
Is like the star them shut they eye,
the country black black the same everywhere.
I can't see me gal,

233

I can't see them man who want to grind me,
I can't see them man I hate. . . .

I seeing faces everywhere I turn,
but they dark dark too dark to mek out,
an' they moving all 'round me, I can't break out,
10 an' St Andrew rise up with Soufriere behind
talking to Pele, and Castries and Roseau;
St George, but him don't have no dragon,
Kingstown don't have no tongue,
it can't say nothing!

15 Don't tell me it going to get blacker.

When me eye close I does see clearer,
an' everything an' everybody does be inside here,
I does see me way clear,
the drums does drive out me fear,
20 the drums does beat in me blood,
(but I know is me heart mekking love),
an' the beat never stop, the rhythm never stop.
The dance in me blood driving me crazy,
the dance in the dark mekking me hop.

25 Oh God! But Satan strong in this place!
In de wake they laughing, in de wedding they wailing,
in de Casino they praying, in de Church they cussing,
an' when they shaking an' they dancing,
is de spirit le' go, jukking for so,
30 an' the passion strip down stone cold naked. . . .

CAMERON KING
St Vincent

Assassins of the Voice

Assassins of conversation
they bury the voice
they assassinate, in the beloved
grave of the voice, never to be silent.
5 I sit in the presence of rain
in the sky's wild noise
of the feet of some who
not only, but also, kill
the origin of rain, the ankle

10 of the whore, as fastidious
as the great fight, the wife
of water. Risker, risk.
I intend to turn a sky
of tears, for you.

MARTIN CARTER
Guyana

To Walter Rodney

Yeah,
you cou'n't o mek it, Walter.
I coulda tell yo so,
but yo never ask.
5 You believe
dat because you born hay,
an pon top o duh
yo damn good at yo job,
dat Guyana
10 woulda tek yo back
in tinks nuttn'.
But yo believe wrong. . .
Remember Rosie Douglas
an de political asylum
15 promise?

Dey gat a word for it, though.
A white-people word.
Pragmatism. . .
An duh's a word
20 dat you shoulda know
since de Shearer time.
But you go an get fool
by a smaller word
than duh.
25 H–O–M–E.

Leh me tell yo, boy.
Home doan mean
wuh you tink it mean.

Home is de yard
30 wheh yo nabel-string bury.

Home is de house
wheh yo wife or yo ol lady
waitin fo yo
wid a hot cup o tea
35 or a nice, steamin plate o food. . .
Duh's home.

An tek it from me, Walter.
Home doan mean
nuttn mo than duh. . .
40 at least
not in Guyana.
Mind yo,
fo some it mean
siren,
45 an outriders,
an banners cross de road.

But fo you
it doan even mean
a job
50 in a university
dat ain nuttn' to dem dat you teach in befo —
even though
a post vacant an you gat de cagaj
and de brain for it. . .

55 Neither it ain mean
groundins wid no brudders,
cause you could grung
wid brudders anyway in dis world
once yo sure yo know
60 who yo brudders really is.

But duh's someting
a lot o people in dis country
ain sure 'bout.
Wuh 'bout you, Walter?
65 You sure
dat yo sure?
No, ah shouldn' ask yo duh:
I sure
dat yo sure now;
70 but I'n so sure
dat yo did sure
before. . .

Anyhow,
ol people seh
75 no cross,
no crown. . .
no goadie,
no grung.

So grung, yeh?
80 Cause d'is goadie time.
An even if
it mean uprootin
one mo time,
yo bound to find
85 anodder home –
not Guyana,
nor Jamaica,
nor Tanzania neither,
but someway far,
90 wheh de road to de university
doan tar
wid politics. . .
someway good,
wheh de only wood
95 yo can hold
is a growin tree. . .
someway ol,
like de Fus'
– or even de Second –
100 world,
wheh dey mus'
vex dat yo black
but gon gie Jack
e jacket anyhow,
105 when it come to tings academic. . .
someway serious,
wheh yo sure dey need
wuh you could gie dem,
an wheh
110 a brain like yours
could able to breathe
at las'. . .

WORDSWORTH McANDREW
Guyana

Two Cultures

'Hear how a baai a taak
Like BBC!
Look how a baai a waak
Like white maan,
5 Caak–hat pun he head, wrist–watch pun he haan!
Yu dadee na Dabydeen, plant gyaden near Blackbush Pass?
He na cut wid sickle an dig wid faak?
He na sell maaket, plantain an caan?
An a who pickni yu rass?
10 Well me never see story like dis since me baan!

E bin Inglan two maaning, illegal,
Eye-up waan-two white hooman,
Bu is wha dem sweet watalily seed
Go want do wid hungrybelly Blackbush weed
15 Like yu, how yu teet yella like dhall
An yu tongue black like casrip!
Dem should a spit, vamit pun yu, beat yu rass wid whip!
Is lungara like yu spoil dem good white people country,
Choke an rab, bruk-an-enta, tief dem people prapaty!

20 So yu tink yu can come hey an play big-shat,
Fill we eye wid cigarette, iceapple an all dat?
Aweh po country people bu aweh ga pride:
Jess touch me gyal-pickni, me go buss yu back-side.'

DAVID DABYDEEN
Guyana

Political Manifestos and Satire

Tomorrow Belongs to the People

Ignorant
Illegitimate,
Hungry sometimes,
Living in tenement yards
5 Dying in burial societies
The people is a lumbering giant
That holds history in his hand.

The efficient engineers dam the conservancies
Design the canals and the sluices
10 The chemists extract their sugar to the ton.

The millers service the padi into rice
And the heavy lorries and unpunctual ships
Bring ground provisions from the farms.

But always the people is a hero, a vast army
15 Making the raw material for skill and machines to work upon.

They frequent the cinemas
Throng the races and the dance halls
Pocket small wages with a sweating brow
And ragged clothes;
20 But it is their ignorant, illegitimate hands
That shape history.

They grow the cane and the rice and the ground provisions
They dig the gold and the diamonds and the bauxite
They cut the forests and build the bridges and the roads and the
25   wall to keep out the sea.

History is theirs,
Because history doesn't belong
To the kings, and the governors and the legislature.
History basically
30 Is the work men do with their hands
When they battle with the earth

And grow food and dig materials
For other people's profits and other people's skill.

And other people know it too.

35 The labour leaders and the politicians
Shake fists to rouse the rabble
But that giant, the people
They say yes or no to the proposition.

Chinese running their groceries and their laundry places
40 Portuguese controlling the dry goods and the pawnshops
Indians saving every half of a shilling
Cutting in canefields
Breaking their backs to grow rice.

Africans tramping aback for the provisions,
45 Running the falls "topside" for fabulous diamonds,
Becoming teachers, the policemen, and the Civil Servants.

They are all heroes,
They make history
They are the power in the land.

50 And the women work patiently along with the men
And look after the children as best they can.

And the children grow
Force their way out of the slums into the professions
And stand up in the legislature.

55 To-day they hope
But to-morrow belongs to the people.
To-morrow they will put power behind their brow
And get skill in their hands.

To-morrow
60 They will make a hammer to smash the slums
And build the schools.

Like a River, the people hold history in their hands
And tomorrow belongs to them.

ARTHUR SEYMOUR
Guyana

Son of Guyana

For John Agard

Doan tell me 'bout Guyana.
I barn deh in t'irty-t'ree.
Meh great-gran'fadda wuz a black man
grandmudda wuz a puttagee.
5 Meh gran'fadda wuz a coolie: ah draw Buck, white an' Chinee.
Deh call it 'land of six peoples'
but is seven, 'less you doan count me.
We had timber, bauxite, diamon' an' gol'.
Sugar wuz king o' de crop,
10 de Union Jack did flyin' pun ev'ry flagpole
an' class deh pun class, so, wid the white man pun top.

Doan' tell me 'bout Guyana.
I wuz a small boy in farty eight
When black police shoot down coolie
15 in de strike at Enmore estate.
Bot' coolie an' black wuz me mattie,
But I din tek it hard.
My fadda had a job in a office
nat in no estate yard.
20 You see,
class de deh pun class, so, wid de white man pun top.

Doan tell me 'bout Guyana. Doan' tell me 'bout old' B G
Deh call it Bookers Guyana
'cause Bookers did own all ah we:
25 estate, grocery, dry goods, drugstore,
even de boats in the sea.
Duh same year wan hell of a fire
bun dung dey biggest shop.
Dey lass piece of dey empire;
30 but you t'ink duh cudda shake t'ings up?
Nah!
Class deh pun class, so, wid de rich man pun top.

Doan tell ME 'bout Guyana! I de deh in fifty-t'ree.
Cheddie an' Forbes win de elections
35 An' we all start feelin' we free.
Chief, Bookers an' dem start fuh trimble;
DEN dey feel dey gine pass fuh grass!
Class start shiftin' pun class, so,
wid de rich man shakin' pun top!

40   Doan tell me 'bout Guyana.
De constitution din' even dry yet
When British tanks roll dung de street;
like wuz some dam' movie set.
de Black Watch soldiers come
45   wid dey big, black boot an' dey gun
an' dey suntan oil an' dey skin fulla boil
to put class back pun class, so, wid de rich man pun top.

Doan' tell me 'bout Guyana.
Nex' election, 'appanjat!' wuz de shout.
50   I de deh in fifty-seven.
Cheddie win without a doubt.
De rich man start prayin' to heaven
an' de CIA start dey campaign.
Soon dey had we killin' each adduh
55   Was 'coolie' an 'niggah' again
while class deh pun class, so, wid de rich man pun top.

Look, chief. DOAN mek joke 'bout Guyana
if you doan want a cuff in you mout'.
I din' really want to leave, you know,
60   ah jus' *feel* ah had to get out.
Ah *hads* wuz to leff Guyana.
Ah leff deh in sixty-one.
Independence wuz a word pun a banner,
an' I didn' black *nor* Indian.
65   Ah start feelin' de strain
a kinda middle-man pain
when class begin mashin' down class, so,
wid de PARTY pun top.

So doan tell me 'bout Guyana.
70   Ah jus doan want to hear.
Doan tell me how t'ings deh so bad now,
every man Jack livin' in fear;
how dey usin' dey head
jus' to ketch a li'l bread
75   and how 'class' like it jus' disappear.
I am a son of Guyana, de lan' dat I love so dear,
Ah swear – to me Gaad! – ah gine back deh,
but, chief, ah cyan' mek it dis year.

MICHAEL GILKES
Guyana

Government Memorandum

With reference to the above
I have the honour
To have been directed
To communicate to you
5 the interim decision of the Board
Pending the approval of the Commission
And subject to such said approval
Which is to say
That what has been said
10 And what is being said
As well as what will be said
Is to be construed as
Until and unless confirmed
By the aforementioned authority
15 With deletions, additions and alterations
As the case may be
Provisional.

Having regard to the nature
Of the discussion held
20 Over the request made
And taking into account
Your field of knowledge
Particularly
Your area of specialization
25 And considering
The degree of your involvement
Not ignoring
Your kind of experience
Nor
30 Your region of residence
I can say with certainty
That the likelihood
Of the possibility
Of giving effect to
35 The matter in question
Seems
In the present circumstances
Probable
In the near future
40 Perhaps.

But in view of
The dire need for Health Educators
And the urgent necessity
To fill these needs

45 As soon as possible
And bearing in mind the foregoing
I have to say
That I am in a position
For the time being
50 To offer you
Tentatively and
Alternatively
The post of
Temporary
55 Supernumerary
Deputy
Assistant
Health Education Officer
Acting
60 In lieu of
The one under reference.

P D SHARMA
Trinidad and Tobago

Per Capita Per Annum

Lesson Five in SEVEN STUDIES IN HOME ECONOMICS
Number of people under review –
91000. Percentage of invisible fathers
or mothers of haphazard status –
79. (or more). Number of people
5   who pay taxes – too many
or too few. Number of people
who starve; number of people who
eat; number of people
who eat people who starve . . .
10   Number of humans, hybrids,
hermaphrodites,
hominids . . .

hogsheads of hate
still wait to be opened
15 *in the headquarters of the hungry*

Number of large heads, spring beds,
large bellies, distended guts, percentage
of placentas per square-inch of a
school-yard; estimate of prostitutes

20   per cubic-centimetre of a cradle.
        Number of beggars, wooden legs,
      scrunters, hunters, highest-
      common-factor of broken skulls
      per milli-litre of strong rum;
25   of broken hearts per man-hour
      of gossip, percentage of
      sheep per driver . . .

in heaven in 1976
there were thousands of suicides
30 *who drank*

Estimates of imports in proportion to bans
  on imports; gross shipping in proportion
  to fishing boats per hundred; cars
  in proportion to arse-holes of population,
35 makes of cars, number of types
  of number-plates of cars.
    Visitors who cannot relate to home,
    divided by tourists who cannot
      pay
40   to leave home.
      Vice against vaccinations,
      lawyers against builders,
      dreams
        against people
45   who cannot sleep . . .

then there was feasting
in the streets of Kush
when the last slave
returned healthy with treasure
50 *from Taiwan*

Percentage of decibels to blossoms;
  number of quiet people, fearless people;
  number of people decently assaulted
  by other people; square-roots of gardens
55 inhabited by paranoid mongrels,
    percentage of poems
    damaged in transport,
    acts of love and labour
    accurately recognisable
60   as pleasure . . .

everyone remembers
not a single song
of the Callinagos

Graphs to indicate the upward and downward
65   curve of arrowroot; segments
            of social circles removed by surgery.
                Emergency graves for the heads
                    of stolen cattle.
                        Straw hats and straw mats;
70   hundreds of people   .
                        with rock-faces fishing for status;
                        9 people fishing
                            with rods on rocks
                            with lanterns
75   ole mas' faces
                                    lights without lustre
                                    crabs . . .

but I could name you
by name
80 *the first Spaniard*
who vomited into his guitar

182000 noseholes under review.
    Hunters and scrunters too many or
        too few. Petites of baby-killing semen;
85   popcorn; sheep
                with number-plates;
                    the downward curve of pigeon-peas,
                        poems, cognition and recognition
                            that died thrashing
90   in an abandoned
                                ambulance . . .

when I was a child
you could buy Aztec soulfood
outside the temples of Niniveh

95 Numbers of numbers –
        bers, bers, bers, – NUMB, – oh so numb . . .
            Exodus, Leviticus, numbers.
                levies, lies, lassitudes . . .

Numberless people under review.
100   Number of THEM – 91000.
        Number of US – 91000.
          Till death
            gives us a head-start –
              per capita
105   per annum
                  every year
                  HERE . . .

    during
    next lesson
110 *Lesson Six*
    those who so wish
    will be taught how to count . . .

                                ELSWORTH KEANE
                                St Vincent

Shaka's Cycle

I   A Light
Brothers and sisters raise the flags
wave the flags of victory. Let the enemy
see red.

5   Today I looked at mama and said,
    mama, today your son will lead his people
    out of this morass

    and mama said go son,
    do what you have to do, but
10 to thy own self be true.

    So here I am this afternoon,
    and already we wave the
    flags of victory.

    Let them know that we are armed
15 we have arms
    we have access to arms.

Let them know that the people are
on the move
let them know that
20 we are on the stage of history
and shall not be moved.

Let them know that this is our
moment of revenge
when we all have
25 to do whatever each man in his heart
thinks most right to be done
about the *atrocities*,
that befell our ancestors in the past.

I am thinking brothers and sisters
30 of all those souls that are lost in
the sea,
lost, cannot return home

cannot ever find land
lost in the Atlantic
35 lost because of the Slave Trade –
a white man invention.
And dat man,
dat man,
(it is definitely impossible to help dat man now)
40 we must haul his tail from whitehall
dat man is responsible for all that we see here today.

We have to deal with that betrayal, We
will deal with it when we make our choice,
and
45 Shaka say the choice is Liberty
or the Cemetery.

Support is growing
the marches are getting bigger
and we all know in our own hearts
50 what we are going to do.
I say no more. No.

When Black people move we
move as one. You know that,
so there is no need for me to say more.
55 We know where the guns are.

We know what to do when
the moment comes

as they say, we have to
seize the time,
60 and time is as tight
as a clenched fist.

II   Burning
So here we are
here we all are.

65 They say it could never have happened
it could not happen
here
it has happened today.

Remember how the heat lashed our foreheads
70 cracked our skulls
how the hot pitch bruised our heels
how our hands cut cane. The march goes on.

We know what we will do. We
know where the guns are. When the time is right
75 we know what to do. The Black man has always
known what to do. Let the drum roll.

So much to be done.
Shaka seldom sleeps. Let the hands of Lakshmi
wave the flags.

80 III   The Final Flame
The question I suppose you are asking
yourselves is where we went wrong. The
question I suppose you are asking yourselves
is how they catch Shaka. The question
85 I suppose you are asking yourselves is
what we do now.

The fight goes on.

Some of the brothers have taken the fight
into the hills. They have taken the matter

90 into their own hands
    and into the hills . . . Each

    in our own heart knows what to do.
    You ask me to speak about
    my feelings,
95 about my experiences in prison.

    I feel too deeply about these
    things,
    to speak of them now. I feel
    too deeply.

100 We need more black sounds.
     Black people know what to do. We
     have always known what to do. Shaka
     say is the fire next time.

                                        VICTOR QUESTEL
                                        Trinidad and Tobago

Voice Portraits

Grandmother

Was once keen-eyed, could thrust
Thread into fine needles without glasses, notice
Miniscule particles of dust
Neglected by housemaids on a high cornice;

5   Was once quick of ear,
Could hear
The footfall of small game in a wood,
Was once as accurate
As most men with guns, more delicate
10 Than most with fishing-rods, good
With club, bat and racquet,
Deadly on the croquet-lawn,
A cool volleyer at the net,
Was once a limber, supple, a dancer into dawn;

15 Was once unwrinkled, smooth,
Nubile, breasts plump with milk
She crooning nippled to the unweaned mouth;

Once thought of taking silk,
Was scholar,
20 Teacher,
President of committees, writer
Of letters to the Press, traveller,
Cook, gardener,
Planner of picnics, holidays, and birthday parties,
25 Teller of fairytales at bedtime, deft binder
Up of cut knees;

Was once confidante, secretary, partner,
And body-servant to the cheeky, wheat-
Headed boy from the house across the street
30 Who broke her first bicycle, became
A good lawyer,
And gave her
Jewelry, four children, his distinguished name
And a respectable collection of mediaeval art;

35   Was once swift, straight, slender,
     Selfless; now all that seems
     Like half-forgotten dreams
     Veiled by head-noises, arthritis, and a weak bladder;

     But clearer than yesterday, and nearer the slowly
          flagging heart
40   Is how once
     (This, only once)
     In a flagrant heat of summer
     She stretched upon the sand
     Her body naked, ripe, unloose,
45   As never now, and
     How matching the intemperate, turbulent brute
     Strength of her dark-haired lover,
     Impenitently she pressed and drained unlawful juice
     Of wild, sweet, timeless fruit.

A L HENDRIKS
Jamaica

God's Work

     Mister Edwards, more my good friend
     Than gardener and handyman at home,
     Served me well for half my life.
     Prince, they called him, born about that colonial time
5   I called him Mister Edwards until the hour he died.

     Strong black face, handsome old man,
     Ashy cap of curled short hair,
     Never sick a day until a day he sick.
     'Wind by the heart', he said
10   But the heart was sound, too sound.
     It took months of agony to kill him
     Ripping his guts away slowly
     Until that strong, good man was nothing.

     'God's work', he would say
15   When the rain pelted down
     And floods rushed in the rivers
     And storms lashed the tree-tops.
     And 'God's work' now he said
     When the pain wracked him

²⁰ Spasms crumpling up his face
Sweat dripping in the effort to hold back
The gut-contracting cry not quite escaping.
'Prince Edwards, he too strong for cry',
But his last day in my arms he cried.
²⁵ 'God's work!'
God should play more.

IAN McDONALD
Trinidad and Tobago

Ganja Lady

The Ganja Lady stands at Halfway Tree
shackled at the neck,
she rolls her eyes, strange
smiles on her lips,
5 in her throat,
days, nights she does not move.

At Papine her justborn child curled to her breast,
sons playing in dirt and grass
the square shimmers, trucks, cars, carts roll past,
10 the child sucks content, the ganja lady stares
her hair unkept, the world oblivious.

Over the wall a face appears
sweet as the moon.
Bogle stares, incredulous with rending hope.
15 The Ganja lady stands at his side
kisses his dry lips, caresses his damp neck.
Bogle gasps, his body drains
its fluids, spews its waste,
she cups the nappy
20 head in her hands, supports
the twisted neck,
eases the lids on his stunned dilated eyes

Nyahman grips the bottle high
tensile, stretched to awesome length, eyes
25 raking the hot street,
'Freedom!' the pose is eternal, carved
in time,
the bottle's venom shards in the street
Ganja Lady mutters: 'Jah! Deliver I!

30 Waist, backside, belly, hips
the drummer smiles, her moves
compel his hands, her feet tattoo
the dust, fire smoulders in her eyes

The goat is bearded, splitting its face
35 a smile, mischievous as old men's memories.
Ganja Lady canters over Babylon
cross-legged, holding the horns, smoke white and
writhing covers her, streams from her locks
her feet, her hands.
40 BongoNyah hears the silent canter
feels its rhythm, sees the Ganja Lady riding
high.
'Jah,' he say, 'Jah!' And smiles.

ROGER McTAIR
Trinidad and Tobago

The Warner Woman

The morning shimmers in its bowl of blue crystal.
Me, underneath my mother's bed.
I delight in dust and dimness.
Connoisseur of comics and the coolness of floorboards,
5 I prolong my life's long morning.

But the blue sky broke. The warner-woman.
bell-mouthed and biblical
she trumpeted out of the hills,
prophet of doom, prophet of God,
10 breeze-blow and earthquake,
tidal wave and flood.

I crouched. I cowered. I remembered Port Royal.
I could see the waters of East Harbour rise.
I saw them heave Caneside bridge. Dear God,
15 don't make me die, not now, not yet!

Well, the sky regained its blue composure.
Day wound slowly down to darkness.
Lunch-time came, then supper-time,
then dream-time and forgetting.

Haven't heard a warner-woman
these thirty-odd years.

EDWARD BAUGH
Jamaica

Kaleidoscope

    Chancellor, the world's
    Mad-music man,
    Danced blithely up the curve
    of his leaping vision,
5   And blew hard.
    Blew blues,
    Blue/black hard.
    Blew hard blues.
    Blew soft blues.
10 Your blues,
    My blues,
    And all God's children's earth bound.
    blues,
    Into God's infinite, receiving sky.

15 And as he blew
    Into the blue/black
    wilderness,
    Of that sweeping
    Cold night sky,
20 A star pitched
    Its way furiously,
    To about ten seconds
    of sheeted green glory.
    And Chancellor stopped
25 dead,
    Frightened at the portent
    of a mad-pitching star.
    As a nervour beggar,
    nearby,
30 Twitched restlessly
    And pitched a ball of spit
    Into the indifferent gutter,
    Running casually down
    the road beside him.

35 Then without fuss
   He put his head sideways,
   Expertly like a hoary old snake.
   And hissing his most venomous
   cuss word at Chancellor
40 For stopping,
   He looked up,
   And began to dream about the stars.

WAYNE DAVIS
Trinidad and Tobago

Absence

How crumpled your clothes look;
soiled and dishevelled
yet suggesting in their lilt
against the basket – something of you;
5 your damp intimate essentials.

Soiled clothes say more than
words. It's you there thrown
aside –
temporarily disembowelled;
10 drooping.

Then comes the hanging
from the clothes line, after
being placed in a wringer.

Frayed, your clothes suggest
15 you are coming to an end.

You have truly suffered. Let me
put my hand in those spaces –
the holes you have vacated.

Slowly,
20 you resurrect every Sunday
when your week's washing is dry.

VICTOR QUESTEL
Trinidad and Tobago

Prince Street

Prince Street is pandemonium
pelting bottle an stone
parting fight
is pedestrians passing
5 an pushing other pedestrians
is pickpockets
pounding on passersby
an pushers in plannings
peddling potent drugs

10 Prince Street is pokerfaced
drunks pretending purity
an prostitutes playing prude
spottyfoot pearl
sparrow sing bout
15 is boys pitching wid girls
boys petting boys
and girls peeping

Prince Street is pissing
on painted walls
20 an walls peeling
is people black people
pacing up an down steps
prying into bars
pssting across pavements
25 is a panorama
of movement an sound

Prince Street is pubs
playing posh
an providing pure funk
30 is man beating man
woman beating pan
washing panties in pools
of putrid water
is a permanent prancing
35 to the popular records
dat spinning

Prince Street is pone eating
pènny sweetbread for ten cents
pans of corn an shutyne
40 an plenty pudding
Prince Street is poorguts

Prince Street is profit
coelho baking pan
numbers selling pants
45 American stores peddling
furniture
Prince Street is poor souls
Prince Street is passive
resistance
50 is part of de plan
to keep Black people in place
is de price paid for being
de prime monster's playground
an Prince Street doesn't beg
55 pardon

Prince Street is
Peter pay for paul
an paul pay for all
is pens an pencils
60 pilfered from poor vendors

Prince Street is
plaiting hair, patting hair
pressing hair, parting hair
painting cheeks, polishing
65 nails
portraying pulchritude
but Prince Street is proud,
positively.
Prince Street is private cars
70 and private taxis
plying routes
wid paying passengers
preachers peeling bells
proscribing poor people
75 Prince Street is eternal pain

Prince Street is petty crimes
then Prince Street is penetrated
is police informers
playing police
80 police passing pay packets
to possible partners
is pigs in plainclothes
parading

police cars patrolling
85   in Prince Street.
Prince Street is pollution
pneumonia an polio
is public punishment

Prince Street is de prototype
90   of Port of Spain
an proof of de poor state
of de entire place
is paradise searching

But Prince Street possesses
95   potential
endless potential
to put an end
to political pressure putters

Its past you can't push aside
100   its present pinches your mind
it was a pathway
to de People's Parliament
before partyhacks
padlocked Prince Street out
105   pity Prince Street
de pariah

Prince Street is
a poem
a play
110   a people's theatre
an it is polemic too

Prince Street is prepared
to partake
in de People's War

115   Power
to the princes an princesses
of Prince Street.

KASI SENGHOR
Guyana

Invitation

I
If my fat
was too much for me
I would have told you
I would have lost a stone
5 or two

I would have gone jogging
even when it was fogging
I would have weighed in
sitting the bathroom scale
10 with my tail tucked in

I would have dieted
more care than a diabetic

But as it is
I'm feeling fine
15 feel no need
to change my lines
when I move I'm target light

Come up and see me sometime

II
Come up and see me sometime
20 Come up and see me sometime

My breasts are huge exciting
amnions of watermelon
                   your hands can't cup
my thighs are twin seals
25   fat slick pups
there's a purple cherry
below the blues
                 of my black seabelly
there's a mole that gets a ride
30 each time I shift the heritage
of my behind

Come up and see me sometime

GRACE NICHOLS
Guyana

260

Granny in de Market Place

Yuh fish fresh?

Woman, why yuh holdin' meh fish up tuh yuh nose?
De fish fresh. Ah say it fresh. Ah ehn go say it any mo'

Hmmm, well if dis fish fresh den is I who dead an' gone
5 De ting smell like it take a bath in a lavatory in town
It here so long it happy. Look how de mout' laughin' at we
De eye turn up to heaven like it want tuh know 'e fate
Dey say it does take a good week before dey reach dat state

Yuh mango ripe?

10 Gran'ma, stop feelin' and squeezin' up meh fruit!
Yuh ehn playin' in no ban'. Meh mango eh no concertina

Ah tell yuh dis mango hard just like yuh face
One bite an' ah sure tuh break both ah meh plate
If yuh cahn tell de difference between green an' rosy red
15 dohn clim' jus' wait until dey fall down from de tree
Yuh go know dey ripe when de lizard an dem start tuh feed
but dohn bring yuh force-ripe fruit tuh try an sell in here
it ehn burglars is crooks like all yuh poor people have to fear

De yam good?

20 Old lady, get yuh nails outta meh yam!
Ah mad tuh make yuh buy it now yuh damage it so bad

Dis yam look like de one dat did come off ah de ark
She brother in de Botanical Gardens up dey by Queens Park
Tourists with dey camera comin' from all over de worl'
25 takin' pictures dey never hear any yam could be dat ole
Ah have a crutch an' a rocking chair someone give meh fuh free
If ah did know ah would ah bring dem an' leave dem here fuh
she

De bush clean?

Well, I never hear more! Old woman, is watch yuh watching meh
30 young young dasheen leaf wit' de dew still shinin' on dem!

It seem tuh me like dey does like tuh lie out in de sun
jus' tuh make sure dat dey get dey edges nice an' brown

an' maybe is weight dey liftin' tuh make dem look so tough
Dey wan' build up dey strength fuh when tings start gettin' rough
35 Is callaloo ah makin' but ah 'fraid tings go get too hot
Yuh bush go want tuh fight an' meh crab go jump outta de pot

How much a poun' yuh fig?

Ah have a big big sign tellin' yuh how much it cos'
Yuh either blin' yuh dotish or yuh jus' cahn read at all

40 Well, ah wearing meh glasses so ah readin' yuh big big sign
but tuh tell yuh de trut' ah jus' cahn believe meh eye
Ah lookin' ah seein' but no man could be so blasted bol'
Yuh mus' tink dis is Fort Knox yuh sellin' fig as if is gol'
Dey should put all ah all yuh somewhere nice an' safe
45 If dey ehn close Sing-Sing prison dat go be the bestest place

De orange sweet?

Ma, it eh hah orange in dis market as sweet as ah does sell
It like de sun, it taste like sugar an' it juicy as well

Yuh know, boy, what yuh sayin' have a sorta ring
50 De las' time ah buy yuh tell meh exactly de same ting
When ah suck an fin' all ah dem sour as hell
De dentures drop out an' meh two gum start tuh swell
Meh mout' so sore ah cahn even eat ah meal
Yuh sure it ehn lime all yuh wrappin' in orange peel?

55 De coconut hah water?

AMRYL JOHNSON
Guyana

Greenidge

Gladiator on the battlefield,
Blading the landscape with an all-conquering sweep,
Lunging limbs jump and jive,
The sword-bat wields, raging
5 A mighty run-running storm
Staging victory;
Islands somersault, spin, full-blooded, bounce,
Shooting fiery eye-balls,

Against a current of robust lashings,
10 Muscles snap!
Players pouncing,
Hairs split
And twine their way to a conquest.
Hearts rip! torn into shreds of strokes,
15 Heads roll! balls are heads where storm-winds reside,
Spectators and players
Beaten into the heroics of God
On the green ridge, smiling;
One man walks a tight-rope,
20 Tightened by a slippery magician.

FAUSTIN CHARLES
Trinidad and Tobago

More Poem

'No more poem!' he raged, eye red;
'A solitary voice is wrong,
Jericho shall fall, shall fall
at the People's song!'

5 So. Only I-tongue have the right
to reason, to that sense of dread.
Man must keep silence now, except
man without bread.

No. See the flesh? It is cave, it is
10 stone. Seals every I away from light.
Alone. Man must chant as Man can
gainst night.

DENNIS SCOTT
Jamaica

Word-Songs

Hymn to the Sea

Like all who live on small islands
I must always be remembering the sea,
Being always cognizant of her presence; viewing
Her through apertures in the foliage; hearing,
5 When the wind is from the south, her music, and smelling
The warm rankness of her; tasting
And feeling her kisses on bright sunbathed days: –
I must always be remembering the sea.

Always, always the encircling sea,
10 Eternal, lazylapping, crisscrossed with stillness,
Or windruffed, aglitter with gold; and the surf
Waist-high for children, or horses for Titans;
Her lullaby, her singing, her moaning; on sand,
On shingle, on breakwater, and on rock;
15 By sunlight, starlight, moonlight, darkness:
I must always be remembering the sea.

Go down to the sea upon this random day
By metalled road, by sandway, by rockpath,
And come to her. Upon the polished jetsam,
20 Shell and stone and weed and saltfruit
Torn from the underwater continents, cast
Your garments and despondencies; re-enter
Her embracing womb: a return, a completion.
I must always be remembering the sea.

25 Life came from the sea, and once a goddess arose
Fullgrown from the saltdeep; love
Flows from the sea, a flood; and the food
Of islanders is reaped from the sea's harvest.
And not only life and sustenance; visions, too,
30 Are born of the sea: the patterning of her rhythm
Finds echoes within the musing mind.
I must always be remembering the sea.

Symbol of fruitfulness, symbol of barrenness,
Mother and destroyer, the calm and the storm!
35 Life and desire and dreams and death
Are born of the sea; this swarming land
Her creation, her signature set upon the salt ooze
To blossom into life; and the red hibiscus
And the red roots burn more brightly against her blue,
40 I must always be remembering the sea.

FRANK COLLYMORE
Barbados

Transition

Watching my wisp of smoke
I know where our dreams go
I know how spirit builds
Pylon and Pyramid
5 Needling receding heaven;
How soul the arrower,
Burster of horizons,
Goes out like hawk and eagle.
Through the star-cluttered night
10 I go where my dreams go.

Come dawn, come sun, come cloud,
Bird-talk, cock-crow, dog-bark;
Men slipping in from sleep
As from another journey
15 Into the inn of day,
Earth turning from nocturne
To morning rhapsody,
My mother island catching
At my heart and feet;
20 I go where my blood goes.

I go where my love goes;
Where the salt sea sprays
Her salt into the blood;
Where my little river
25 Runs rhythms out to sea;
Where the green hills' tower
Stands against the sky
Where in fertile valley

Grand, green fields of corn
30 Preach of splendid harvests.

Here in my huddled village
Blood pulses into blood;
Kinsman hallos kinsman;
Deep-bosomed women gossip
35 From dooryard into dooryard
And children scamper barefoot
Ah, there the heart gold goes
Slender as a young palm,
Comelier than Sheba
40 Golden in young sun.

ERIC ROACH
Trinidad and Tobago

Flute(s)

For Pam Mordecai

Its when the bamboo from its clip of yellow groan and wrestle
begins to glow and the wind learns the shape of its fire

and my fingers following the termites drill
find their hollows of silence . shatters of echoes of tone

5 that my eyes close all along the wall . all along the branches . all
along the world

and that that creak and spirits walking these graves of sunlight
spiders over the water . cobwebs crawlng in whispers over the
stampen green

10 find

from a distance so cool it is a hill in haze
it is a fish of shadow along the sandy bottom

that the wind is following my footsteps
all along the rustle all along the echoes all along the

15 world

and that that stutter i had heard in some dark summer freedom
startles and slips from fingertip to fingerstop
into the float of the morning into the throat of its sound

it is a baby mouth but softer than the suck it makes
it is a hammock sleeping in the woodland
it is a hammer shining in the shade

it is the kite ascending chord and croon and screamers.
it is the cloud that curls to hide the eagle
it is the ripple of the stream from bamboo

it is the ripple of the stream from blue
it is the gurgle pigeon dream the ground dove coo
it is the sun approaching midday listening its splendour

it is your voice alight with echo . with the birth of sound

20

25

EDWARD KAMAU BRATHWAITE
Barbados

Mulatta Song

Very well Mulatta,
this dance must end.
This half-arsed band
blowing its own
5   self-centred song.
The bass slack stringed
slapped by some wall-eyed
mother's son.
This session must done
10   soon done.
O how you danced Mulatta
to the music in your head
pretending that their notes
were your notes.

15 Till the gateman whispered
   into the side of your head
   'Mulatta, mulatta, that's the
   dance of the dead'.
   So you rubadub and rentatile
20 and hustle a little
   smiling the while
   pretending that
   this terrible din
   is a well tuned air
25 on a mandolin.
   And Mulatta your red dress
   you wore here as new
   is a wet hibiscus
   what will you do?
30 Fold the petals of the skirt
   and sit this last long
   last song out.
   Bind up the blood-wound
   from the heart on your sleeve
35 And now Mulatta it's time to leave.

LORNA GOODISON
Jamaica

Ungod on The Day of the Egg

   ungod on
   the day of the egg
   may you come
   the light comes on
5 the valley of cries

   up from the sea
   the egg rises
   into the air
   the piano note
10 crosses it quickly as

   light   the light spilling
   downward all day
   I have given you voice
   said the egg   I have given
15 you ash said the egg

I have given you music
the bell rang it out
the pebble slipped up
the nightingale sang it
20 the piano kissed darkly

I came on the face
in the last church
it is air air
swinging beside us
25 the music inside me

all day
I had wanted poems like these
the valley recrossed me
I fell on my hands as
30 the cries rose

ANTHONY McNEILL
Jamaica

For the Sax Player

clear music spiral – sound in flight
aztec birds swift through early forests,
stream moving heavy spreckled gold
molten subterranean metals
5 i hear you man
calling out through space and time
rich, rich gift blowing out the soul
high and wide, sweet travel
mind in flight
10 swirling lucid tones
so near to
the center
man you give me happiness
for pure whole measures
15 of liquid time.

CHRISTINE CRAIG
Jamaica

Carnival

The Silk Cotton tree
Dances breast-plated in rainbow-plumes
Into the arms of the tuning bamboo
Masked as a boa-constrictor
5 Leaping in feathers of Red Indian head-dress
Swinging, branch rhythm curling pan-sounds
Punching jumping yam-roots
Wild in the motions of a breadfruit band
Garlanded in gold and silver, trunk reeling
10 Star-faces of parakeets in a sea of sailors
Coming in battling green
As the sky bursts
Into hawk-spray, raining yellow and red
Turning crimson onto beaten brass;
15 The hibiscus rises,
Sparkles into a diamond
Then waves a magic wand
Changing the prancing mongoose
Into an agouti with wings;
20 The Silk Cotton sings,
Beating a ringing melody
Through the heart of the bacchanalian forest;
The wild deer is a conquistador,
Threading sunlight with a spider's web;
25 Trees drumming, the road-march pulling,
Vines twanging tambourines
Spinning the blackbird's head;
The blooming blast of trumpet-flower
Turns a red monkey on its head,
30 Winding into an emerald, jigging
In a purple-velveted squirrel,
Rolling in vermilion;
Bush-feet slap, branches clap,
Swirling a copper-helmet beaded in rhine-stones;
35 The boar's grunting bronze
Blows ribbons of pink satin
On flamingoes clutching
A tiara of sea-green butterflies;
Harmonic winds caress the world-creating jungle,
40 The armadillo's gong electrifies
A glitter of peacocks coming through mango blossom
Plucking the humming strings
Of guava-flower ripening into samba;
Waves of coconut-palm cymbals clashing

45 Immortelle waving a banner;
   The rolling hills chime mahogany,
   Steel chords clanging sweet
   With gold floating on air
   And green smiling romance
50 Embracing a crowned serpent.

                    FAUSTIN CHARLES
                    Trinidad and Tobago

Index of Poems

Index of poems by author